STEPPING AROUND
THE COWCATCHER

A Minneapolis Childhood

HENRY T. GALLAGHER

ISBN: 978-1-5487-3692-7

Cover photographs: Streetcar on Selby–Lake line;
1951 City Hockey (Cub Division) champs, Minnehaha Falls Athletic
Club (see page 88 for list of names); Arloine Dolan, with author
(Hiawatha Elementary School graduation, 1951); Minnehaha Falls.

Disclaimer: My parts of this story were written as I best recall
them, letting my imagination fill in the gaps. In so doing, I did not
intentionally fictionalize or distort. However, some names
and biographical details have been altered to protect the innocent.

For all those in our 1957 graduating class
who have "gone ahead."

Now, no more alleys to go down

and backyards to go into, up to a door

to ask the apron-wearing woman

behind the screen,

"Can Bobby come out and play?"

Now, no more alleys,

no more apron-wearing woman.

Preface

Childhoods are lived only once, but are remembered many times and in many different ways. Often the "as lived" and "as remembered" versions are far apart; sometimes they're so close they fall into each other's laps. Writing *Stepping Around the Cowcatcher*[1] was an attempt at catching more of the "lived," but I also settled for the "remembered," knowing full well the fog of memory.

I began to write pieces of this story ("memoir" being too presumptuous a word, laden with reader expectations seldom met) beginning in 2000. I had been living "out east" when a childhood friend called and urged me to come back to my hometown to join a group of former high school classmates for a weekend of golf and fishing up north. But for a few short visits to aging parents, and one or two high-school reunions, it had been 40 years since I'd left the state. While I seldom engaged in either sport, I decided to take part in what had become, for them, an annual event on a Canadian island on the Lake of the Woods.

After that first trip back, one of the group suggested I write something about seeing old friends after such a long absence. I wrote a few comments and put them in the form of a memo. (What else would a lawyer do?) In sequels over the next few years, I expanded the scope of the pieces to include our shared childhood in south Minneapolis.

---

[1] A cowcatcher is a device attached to the front of a streetcar or locomotive in order to clear obstacles off the track.

Eight editions later, I thought that someday I might want to revisit sections of the memos and weave them together into some coherent form, ending with a memory piece about growing up in the 1940s and '50s. It would be a "Wonder Years" kind of story, say, from ages seven to fifteen. (I had no interest in what happened to us after we set foot in the hallways of our high school.)

The sections extracted were limited to the horizons of my boyhood wanderings, my "kid blocks" only. Surely, kids from the two other junior-high neighborhoods had memories of their own. I needed to hear from their "voices."

And they had the time to speak up. We all were at a point in our lives when things had slowed down a bit, when retirement was the only thing to get up for in the morning. We had time on our hands. The kids were long gone. And if any of *their* kids came through the door they usually didn't stay the night. Book clubs, golf clubs and a few trips to Glacier or Hawaii were pretty much it. But there was the Internet.

I sent solicitation letters to a sampling of former classmates asking for childhood memories:

> *I have yet to settle on a kind of model inquiry/questionnaire format that will evoke the memory pieces ... school playgrounds, Park Board boxes in the summer, backyards, end of WWII, "up at the lake," summer vacations, Lake Nokomis, alleys, woods, Minnehaha Falls, Lake Street, trips downtown, streetcars, churches, religious-instruction classes, Sundays, cars, comic books, Saturday morning serials, and on and on.*

I added,

Maybe I'll touch on some darker issues as well: race, anger management, bipolar behavior (before we even knew), alcoholic parents (if relevant to children in the house), child abuse (suspected), petty crime, fights, shy kids (depression?), bullies, deaths, and the polio epidemic.

At first I was afraid I might run across one or two former classmates who didn't wish to journey back and open up parts of their childhoods that might be uncomfortable for them. Perhaps they had left those memories in a pile down on the basement floor of their childhood homes, boarded them up and fled off toward adulthood. That was not the case.

The initial responses, though honest and forthright, were a bit tentative and predictable (read: "Happy Days" anecdotes). "My childhood block … was a dream, one block north of Minnehaha Parkway" and "Growing up in the '40s and '50s was wonderful; completely different from the experiences our grandchildren have today." I had to reread my letter to make sure I hadn't asked for "only the good times, please, if you don't mind?"

Young lives back then included as many dark periods and troubling episodes as the lives of kids today. They just weren't talked about as much, if at all. Late last year, I urged the story-tellers to dig a bit deeper. In so doing, I didn't want to show disrespect for the reputed stoic (some would say "tight lipped") traditions in my Scandinavian south Minneapolis. But I mentioned that I'd been living out east in a vibrant cross-section of American diversity, where, at the drop of a hat, childhood memories are recalled (both the light and the grim stuff).

Nor did I mean to imply that Minnesotans didn't have opinions or make judgments. Of course, they do! But they often don't share them with others. A few years ago, I met a transplanted Minnesotan here in Washington, D.C., who corrected me when I mentioned the expression "Minnesota Nice." He said, "No. Nice has nothing to do with it. It's Minnesota Polite."

The subsequent responses were encouraging. Other stories started to come in — self-conscious kids (boys and girls) in seventh-grade gym classes, alley and playground bullies, racial slurs, a family member's mental depression, childhood obesity issues (classmate teasing), "dirty old man" accounts, an alcoholic father's theft of a son's paper route money, a neighbor's suicide, and more. In short, real life.

In addition to the numerous email submissions I received, I supplemented my research by making three trips back to Minneapolis to conduct "up close and personal" interviews.

Early into the project I realized that, while many of us did not know each other at the time, we shared common experiences. We 1939 babies were, for the most part, cut from the same cloth. A lot of us cried on our first day of kindergarten, played kick the can, pretty much didn't know where babies came from, and were thrilled to be making money on our first jobs.

In addition to the candid, warm and humorous submissions that I received in response to my solicitation letter "from out of your past," I was delighted to get (unexpectedly) what I'll simply call thank-you notes. I knew that I was onto something.

> "Thank you for including me in this project. I haven't thought of my classmates for so many years, and many of them I only knew casually at best. Now I feel close to them all, hurting because they hurt and sad for so many who are gone, and thankful they were in my life, even marginally, so many years ago."

> "I love the way your project has gotten me thinking about fading memories that might have completely disappeared but for your questions."

> "I have been surprised at how much I'm enjoying looking back at those years, something that wasn't really important to me until you challenged us to think back and keep digging. I'm thinking this memoir will do the same for most of the class when it's finished."

> "Love your thoughts in the book ... should be wonderful to read."

> "What fun it's been to be part of your endeavor from incubation on ... can't wait for the compiled fruits of your labor."

This story has a lot of tellers. Twenty-nine, if my final count is right. I hope that I have done a good job of weaving their stories into mine. The larger story then became ours. It was but a representative sampling of anecdotes that others, whom I did not reach, might end up calling their own as well.

The names of the storytellers will be recognizable. I've used the same names that were on small cards pinned to their shirts and dresses when they first set foot in kindergarten across south Minneapolis, that September in 1944. While today they might be known as Jorun Robillard, Jane Hess or Joanne Haugen, back then they were Jorun Olson, Jane Hagen and Joanne Mahre. In *Cowcatcher,* I have held out for those maiden names. (The full list of storytellers is in the "Acknowledgments," which includes the married names of women.)

I have reconstructed certain scenes in *Cowcatcher* from my best recollections. I walked through the same mental fog that most of the tellers did, but we got the bigger picture right, if not the small details over in the corners. Some of the characters are from my imagination, present in the story to carry the narrative with me. For example, my pal Bobby ("four garages up") is a composite of two or three childhood "best" friends.

In the case of some of the submitted anecdotes (and some of my own) I exercised the disclaimer from my initial letter: "No names if it causes shame, embarrassment or sadness for a former classmate or his family." I'm simply trying to shed light on our times — growing up in the 1940s and '50s — the very purpose of the project. It is the episode that mattered, not the actor or actors.

I put that disclaimer to good use in one instance for selfish reasons. I was advised by one storyteller that I might not want to expose the real identities of a childhood bully or bullies. I agreed. It may be a matter of embarrassment to them or their offspring. But such disclosures might also generate acts of revenge. I didn't want any of their grandchildren to come out to Washington, D.C., and shoot out my porch light.

So there you are. When I first started this project, I thought it might be quite a challenge. And it was! But once I got into it, I thought, "What a wonderful ride this is!" Thanks, in large part, to those who came forward willingly, honestly and with humor — not to help me write my story, *but to write theirs*. I can only hope that you enjoy the ride as much as I did.

You can go back to a time before we became cynical, opinionated and intolerant. To a time when our view of life was as fresh and pure as the water that ran over the stones in the creek that came over from Minnetonka — before it got to the dirty waters of the Big River. When we were still children, standing apron-high to a mom at a kitchen sink who answered, "No" and then went searching for a reason after we asked, "Why?"

A final note. My classmates might think that I wrote this book for them. Not exactly. I (and the storytellers) wrote these stories to pass on to their grandchildren. These are pieces of family histories that might otherwise never have reached them.

I began my story in an alley in the voice of the boy I once was. I hope that I remained faithful to him — and to you, the reader, all the way to the end — to the lobby of the Gopher Theatre.

Introduction

It's a few years into the 21st century, and I'm on an early-morning flight from my Washington, D.C., home to Minneapolis. My return trips to the Twin Cities have become infrequent since Mom passed away in 1981 and Dad came to live with us in 1984.

It's a Northwest ("We're not happy until you're not happy") flight that circles around to land from the west, which gives me a chance to locate city landmarks out the window. I'm able to see the skyscraper of the 1920s, the Foshay Tower. Its reputation has been downsized since the 1970s, when others (like the IDS Tower) more befitting a modern downtown began to appear.

Once I see Lake Calhoun I glance at Lake Harriet, and then we're over Nokomis and Hiawatha on the left. I try to spot my old neighborhood, but the plane is falling fast. I can only catch the tall flour mill at the railroad tracks on Hiawatha and then walk my eyes down 42nd Street to the river.

We're over Fort Snelling Cemetery now. All the white grave markers are standing at attention in the bright morning sun. John Pollard, Butch Born and Doug Nash — three who wore our country's cloth — are down there. The Navy was unable to recover the remains of Marlow Madsen and Paul Carlson in the waters off Vietnam. Their names are only on The Wall in Washington, D.C., along with the rest who served and never came back.

On the ground moments later: "Welcome to the Twin Cities of Minneapolis and St. Paul. Local time is 9:17 a.m. Central Daylight Time. Thank you for choosing Northwest."

I'm grateful once again that the tower personnel were on the job, giving the pilots landing instructions. Proof that not everyone in Minneapolis, this summer morning, is "up at the lake." And I know that we've landed at the right place — the Scandinavian city of my birth. The public address system is paging an "Arvid Berglund," and I meet a parade of blond hair and blue eyes coming toward me on Concourse F. (I'm convinced that brunettes have to wait longer for their bags to come off the carousel downstairs.)

I look up at the corrugated ceiling of blown concrete and wonder which sections Terry Baxter, Dave Kahn and I worked on as carpenter helpers and construction laborers for Foley Brothers in those summers of '57 and '58, after high school.

With no bags to claim on my one-day turnaround trip I walk over to an adjoining parking garage to pick up a rental. I usually can't remember the name of the car I've ordered, because it's no longer the name of the manufacturer but of an animal or bird — an impala or pinto, a skylark or a sunbird. The demeanor of the counter guy is pleasant and friendly, not a line item in his job description. I'm once again reminded of the phrase I hear "out east" about the characterization of the people from my home state: "Minnesota Nice."[2]

Like a lot of drivers with rentals, I seldom work the dash-board dials and operational knobs and buttons before I drive off.

---

[2] Yes, Minnesota Polite is a better fit. I believe that some Minnesotans, like many Americans in the rest of the country, may be judgmental, but a Minnesotan will keep it to himself.

I look at them as accessories. Later. Only when I find out that they're essentials — lights, windshield washers and turn signals — does the quick fiddling come. And once on, how do I turn them off? On overnight trips, I've been known to peek out from behind the curtains of my hotel room before going to bed, hoping that the headlights on my rental have finally gone off.

As I turn off a ramp onto dual highways 5 and 494 toward the Mendota Bridge, I elbow my small two-door sedan into a lane. Up ahead a truck is using its shoulders to do the same, as we join a slow-moving car train. Many of the drivers probably wish they were still up at the lake and not part of this morning's crawl hour. Odd that traffic people on the radio still call it a "rush hour."

For a second, my eyes suddenly lock onto a Minnesota license plate on the car ahead. I catch myself and realize that I'm here.

I'm on the Highway 100 of my childhood — the Beltline. When I was on this road in my kid days, I knew we were really going someplace and not just over to Aunt Ethel's off Chicago Avenue by the creek. (Aunts. At first, I didn't know how I got to have them or where they came from. Growing up, I had three of them. It never occurred to me that a mom would have a sister — only that kids had aunts.) We could get to Aunt Ethel's house by going straight west on 42nd Street and over a few avenues, but not by a highway.

Once my dad had the car on this road, it meant we were going someplace to have fun. There was that time when John Pollard and his folks had a Fourth of July picnic with my family. It was on a concrete picnic table at one of those WPA-built roadside parks along the Beltline. He came in his dad's '38 Terraplane, my brother and I in our '39 Chevy. I went home that day without Aunt Ethel's lipstick all over my face.

I try the radio. It has a console of buttons that would trip up a veteran airline pilot. Pushing them becomes a crap shoot. I miss the dials that used to move back and forth along a line of stations. Now, we're all-digital, and we don't dial anything anymore. We punch out or key in. But I do try the radio to catch an East Coast baseball score from last night. I come upon a commercial, "...so when the moment comes, you can be ready..."; I move on to "...if you have black circles or bags around your eyes...." I cut it off but come upon a batch of five commercials, each sixty seconds long, one of which asks, "Are you urinating more frequently?"

I give up. No, this is not the WCCO or KSTP of my childhood. Even a farm report from Maynard Speece would be welcome: "Out Hook 'Em Cow Way," in South St. Paul, telling us about pork bellies. Even that would've been a relief from the madness of the commercials. Howard Viken and Jergen Nash, where are you?

I turn off at the Highway 55 exit, onto Hiawatha Avenue. (As a kid I didn't know that Hiawatha had a number.) Minnehaha Park is coming up on the right. On the left is our old swimming hole in the creek. Down there — where it pooled up against the small dam before continuing on its way over to the Falls — Butch, Jimmy Carlson, Pollard and I would go when we were too lazy on those hot afternoons to ride our stripped-down bikes over to Nokomis.

There's no overhead railing on a bridge to look over and down at the creek. There's no bridge. Hiawatha and a light-rail track now run under Minnehaha Parkway. No pedestrian access. An approaching train passes me. I turn left at the last corner and park as close as I can to the south side of the creek, Gerry Bingham's side.

I work my way toward a swampy smell, pushing through rotting weeds beyond the backyard of someone's creek-side house. I smile and tell the curious (read: suspicious) guy standing in the yard that I'm looking for my childhood. He has a puzzled look and doesn't return my smile. I should've said, "Plainclothes, MPD Missing Persons Bureau, Sir ... looking for one of them."

I feel a sense of anticipation. I can see the water now. I slip-slide down toward a concrete embankment along the creek, an almost seventy-year-old man trying to hold onto two slippery tree branches, his balance and his memories. I get to the edge and look across. There it is. I stare down at the water and try to bring it all back. The cast-iron railing that we jumped from is gone, as is the tree with its huge branch that stretched out over the water. So too are Butch and Pollard. We'd tie a rope and swing from it before we fell into the creek with boy-fun abandon. The only remains of the old Hiawatha Avenue Bridge are stumps of its foundation sticking up from the water, like the barnacled skeleton of some sunken ship.

The creek that has flowed uninterrupted under all the city bridges stops finally and pools up here, as it did then. But it's black, brackish-looking now. To dive into it would require a lot of kid-courage and a tetanus shot. The dark water waits its turn to go down the small spillway, speed up again and slip under another bridge complex, carrying the other Indian-named avenue of my childhood, Minnehaha. Despite the overhead noise of another passing train and the car traffic that should've disturbed the moment, it's somehow quiet down here. And a little sad. I don't know why. I guess the word is melancholy.

Back on top, I look over at the former location of Mr. Longfellow's library. Now the no-longer-books building has been moved a few blocks east to the edge of the park. It's on the former site of the pony-ride concession, where my brother and I broke a few broncos in our time. I had graduated to the live ones; before then, I had ridden the fake ones on the merry-go-round over at Powderhorn on the Fourth.

I should get back to the car before Mr. Backyard Curious goes out front and calls in my license plate.

Moments later I turn into the park, having passed a restaurant that was once the Canteen. After I was old enough to know what "hang out" meant and how to do it, we often went there.

On late nights we sat and ate fried, overly-breaded pork-on-a-bun sandwiches wrapped in aluminum foil. We drank malted milks and plugged nickel after nickel into the booth-side juke box, and kept pushing the smudged and worn D5 button to hear "Sha-boom, Sha-boom," and B-7 to hear the Crew Cuts tell us one more time that "…life could be a dream!" Then there was Kitty Kallen and Teresa Brewer. All the while, Butch would be out in the parking lot picking a fight with somebody.

I park the car near the small train station they've kept and walk back over to try to find where my line of sight of the creek's flow into the park stopped. Weeds hide rusted rails from the old freight train bridge. I glimpse the water and trace its flow, now fast moving again as it passes in view of Mr. Hiawatha, son of Wenonah and grandson of Nokomis, on a statue carrying the fair Dacotah maiden, "Laughing Water" Minnehaha, and continues on its way over the cliff.

Ah! *The Song of Hiawatha.* Legend has it that this brave Indian chieftain demanded that the white settlers erect a statue of him and his wife on this spot. He went further and insisted that they name their parks and woodlands, golf courses and lakes, as well as their schools, avenues and churches, after the two of them, and while they were at it, his mother and grandmother. If they failed to do so, he threatened to go on the warpath with a raiding party that would lay waste the lands of this corner of south Minneapolis — including the Dairy Queen — rendering it even flatter than it already was.

I go into the park, a second playground for so many of us, walk over to the low stone wall, and stare at the cascade of water coming down and right into the camera of the man standing next to me, a tourist. I think he was from Sweden, the country that's a cousin of Minneapolis.

The memories. Dickie and I would relay a red rubber ball over the waterfall on summer days. He threw it into the stream above while I stood down below at the creek's edge — by the little stone bridge — to retrieve it. It was his turn at other times to pluck it out of the water and run up the wide stone steps, where I met him halfway down and grabbed it, turned around, and rushed back up to do it all over again. Late into those afternoons. Then one day, though I was able to catch a flash of red riding down the crashing white foam, I lost the ball as it rushed down-stream toward me. It went bouncing and surging over the stones and rocks on its way past the Deer Pen and out into the Big River, the "Father of Waters."

That night, I was sad — and yet excited — when I went to sleep wondering how far the ball had gone. Red Wing? Even as far as Iowa? Or, maybe it got pulled loose from a snag and traveled farther down the river and out into an ocean. The next morning, I got out my dad's *Rand McNally* and followed my finger as I traced the Mississippi down to a place called New Orleans.

Now, as I cross the street and walk toward the pavilion, I look around. What's wrong with this picture on a kid's-school-vacation morning? I see them either getting off buses in chaper-oned bunches or arriving in vans driven by grown-ups. But no kids just with other kids, playing up top here or down below along the creek. Maybe down in the Deer Pen as well. We never came down here on field trips.

I enter the open-air building and squint as I try to walk my memory back. How cool and dark it was that first day so many years ago when I went into the big high-ceilinged hall, as high up as the ceiling at St. Helena's church, I remember thinking. Sugary smells swirled from the cotton candy and ice-cream concessions at the counters on the far side. I walked across the wide expanse of the floor, little kid steps, to get there. My eyes locked onto the revolving shiny metal bars that kept going around and around inside a lighted glass case of a taffy-pulling machine.

I remember that day. I hurried past the cotton-candy lady to the next counter and asked for an ice-cream sugar cone. Not the tasteless vanilla-wafer kind that came prepackaged in boxes in the freezer chest at Guptil's on 42nd but the dark brown, waffled, hard-crusted kind. (Those wax-papered Drumstick cones came later, but no, not the same.) A tall woman — I guess they all were — behind the counter asked me where I got my red hair. I tried not to be distracted by the question. I didn't answer. She smiled and asked what flavor I wanted. She was patient. She knew that I was flying solo, no parent shadowing me, and that I wanted to get it right. I blurted out, "vanilla" and put my dime on the counter. She saw it and knew that I meant business.

Now, so many years later, I go out through a back door onto the grounds and walk toward a spot amid a huge stand of oak trees. I glance up toward Nawadaha Boulevard and try to retrieve childhood scenes. Too fleeting, but I catch one. A green-painted wooden structure once stood here. I can't remember if cooking stoves were inside, but a lot of women with aprons over their cotton dresses worked at tables crowded with food in glass jars, in pans, on dishes and in covered bowls. I moved closer to them. They spoke a language I couldn't understand.

That day, maybe it was in 1947, men in chairs up on a wooden bandstand were playing musical instruments. Grown-ups sat on blankets and at picnic tables; others were throwing horseshoes while kids ran around playing on swings and monkey bars. I found out that it was Swedish Day ("Svenskarnas Dag") in the park. (The Norwegians would get their day a few Sundays later.) I wondered if we had a day. My mom had told me that we were Irish.

But one of the strongest Minnehaha Park memories I have is that of a Fourth of July celebration, possibly a year later. I won the freckle contest. A WWII veteran in a uniform covered with ribbons presented me with the top prize, a shiny silver dollar. Dick Kreider (who punted footballs barefooted for Augsburg) was second, and my brother was third. I walked home down 44th, and from time to time, I'd put my hand in my pocket and squeeze my folded hankie until I could feel the hard coin.

The day after my big win, the *Minneapolis Star* called my mom and said they were going to send a reporter out to the Hiawatha playground the next day to take a photo of me — holding a rabbit. That morning I got up early, put on a brand new T-shirt and went across the street. I waited. And waited. Neither the reporter nor the rabbit showed. My first introduction to an unreliable press.

Now, I walk back to the car and drive over to Hiawatha, going north, passing the ghost of Charlie's drive-in. As I approach a red light at 42nd, the street my eye had tracked from the plane, I sense a flashback off to the right. It's Bruce McKusick and me crossing the railroad tracks on our way home from St. Helena's Sunday school. I turn right at the corner and continue driving into my memories, the working-class neighborhood of my childhood.

I pass Snelling and Dight, the two avenues of the former tight-knit community of black families (L.C. Hester's being one) in houses up along the railroad tracks from 35th to 38th. I did not realize until years later that they were allowed to settle on those few blocks at the nod of red-lining mortgage lenders downtown — shoehorned into an enclave surrounded by our all-vanilla-white neighborhood. When the Dye brothers (RHS '55 and '56) and their sister Denise (RHS '57) moved into a house at 3636 Minnehaha Avenue in the late '40s, they were but steps outside the red line. On their move-in day, shouting and jeering protesters gathered on nearby lawns and across the street. Fearing violence, their father made the kids sleep on the kitchen floor for the first few nights, while all the white kids up and down the street slept in their beds.

Nor did I realize that when the blacks wanted to go downtown to the RKO Pan or Gopher theaters on Hennepin, they had to sit up in the balconies, directed there by flashlight-waving ushers. Probably wouldn't even have been allowed inside Bridgeman's ice-cream parlor next to the theater.

Two more blocks on 42nd and there's Francis "Lady Kemp Ice Cream" Drugs at Minnehaha, then down the only hill of my childhood, past Jane Hagen's house and Vince "Golden Gloves" Donnelly's. Then, Arloine Dolan's avenue, Janet (clarinet-playing) Solberg's house, and Roy Jensen's (Bev Lusian's husband), his with the water pump in the backyard. The corner grocery store,

Guptil's, then down past Pollard's and mine. I look down 42nd toward Gary Howard's house and Paul Carlson's, all the way to the river.

I park the car at the tennis courts across from my house on 44th. I find myself standing back against the fence. The elms that once shaded the backyard and south side of our corner house are gone. Killed — every last one of them — when the Dutch sent their elm disease on a drive-by sweep through the city in the 1960s. The house looks so small. I stare at it. Squinting now — at the dining room window. No sign of the wide, wooden Venetians.

I hold the squint a little longer and then open my eyes wide. OK, I get it. I'm back.

I see a redheaded, freckle-faced kid slam-bang out a back screen door into the first day of his summer vacation. He'll be twelve years old in a month. He runs across a scuffed-grass back-yard, opens a crooked-hanging gate that once again scrapes out a white quarter-circle on the concrete sidewalk, continues past his dad's car resting in the driveway, and turns at the corner of the garage into the alley to meet Bobby, who's coming down to meet him. Bobby's house is four garages up.

PART I

1

"I heard them when I was still in bed!" Bobby was out of breath.

"Yeah, let's go!" We turned and came back out of the alley and started to run up the street.

I had jumped up from the breakfast nook by the window when I first heard the noise. It had broken the morning calm and was getting louder. *They* were coming closer.

"Finish your — "

"I will, Mom, I'll be back." I ran to my room, laced on my U.S. Keds and came back through the kitchen. I grabbed a couple of vanilla wafers from an opened carton next to the bread box and banged open the back screen door into the yard.

My mom shouted something through the screen window. I couldn't hear her as I ran around my dad's car and into the alley. Maybe it was something about remembering — to wash my hands after, or zip up, or make my bed or brush up and down not sideways, or put the cap back on the toothpaste or the cap back on anything. I was never a good "put back" or "pick up" kid. At that age I thought a lot of that stuff was what moms were for.

They were about four blocks away. First, the tractor with the huge steel claw, banging and jerking its way down 42nd toward my house — digging and gouging up clumps of the street.

Sweet-smelling tar, "street licorice." The driver was being thrown side-to-side in a strapped-in seat as he sat atop the angry bull.

Then, shouting, sweating, sunburned workers followed with their yellow road rollers, graders, and black oiler trucks. The line of vehicles clattered down from Minnehaha Avenue. For small boys with big eyes, it was as good — the noise and the smells — as any circus parade.

John Pollard's cocker spaniel dashed out into the street. Trixie tried to bark away the big machines that were closing on and terrorizing her house. Excited children, hypnotized by the moment, trailed after the modern-day Pied Pipers — all the way down to the river.

Elephants were the only missing piece.

For a few of those summers, we couldn't follow the work crew all the way to the river. They would go too close to Sheltering Arms, the orphanage-turned-hospital. We'd get polio — my mom said — if we went near the building behind the trees. That's where kids, crippled by the virus, lay in beds out on the porches, struggling for air. Others were inside, trapped in breathing machines called iron lungs.

We left the parade at 45th, by Paul Carlson's and Gary Howard's (RHS '56), and went back up the street to Guptil's grocery across from our grade school. A tiny brass bell on the door announced our arrival with a "cling, cling." Mrs. Guptil came out from her family's apartment in the back.

I dunked my arm into the ice-cold water of the cooler and drew up a Dr. Pepper. Yanked off the cap at the screwed-in opener on the cooler — no need for a church key. I placed the cap in my pocket for the streetcar track later that day. Or to add to my collection for the checkers game if we didn't have enough. I always played my caps down, the other kid, caps up. My ritual; my good luck.

I lifted one of the top doors of the steel chest and pulled out a Fudgsicle. The wrapper was cold in my hand. I grabbed the stick. Bobby got a Coke and chocolate buttons on a long sheet of white paper. We put our coins down on the counter. Before we reached the door, Bobby was already running his teeth down the strip. All this under the smiling — and watchful — eyes of Mrs. Guptil.

Once out on the sidewalk Bobby grabbed his bottle by its neck and slugged the pop down, then wiped his mouth with the back of his hand. Just like the whiskey-drinking bad guys — Black Bart and his gang — in the cowboy serials on Saturday mornings. Hopalong wore black, too, but his horse, Topper, was all white.

We crossed the street and went around the back of our one-story grade school. We had just graduated from Hiawatha.

Hiawatha Elementary School, 1951. Courtesy Carolann (Hendrix) Lavell.

A hallway door on the kindergarten side was open. The janitor had just come up to it, maybe taking a break. The smell of new floor wax came with him.

"Mind if we look inside, Mr. Swenson?"

"Take those shoes off and stay on the newspaper if you want to come in."

"Thank you, sir."

I looked over at Bobby. "Finish your pop so we can go in."

"I thought you two had enough of this place."

We went in. "Mr. Swenson, Bobby here thinks he flunked sixth grade and has to come back in September."

"No, now, I saw both of you on Ribbon Day," his Swedish sprinkling over his English, "standing out there with your arms around the girls, photos and all." He looked at Bobby. "Young man, you know Mrs. Gruver would not let you do that if they had to hold you back."

I looked around. Peeked into the kindergarten room. Ah, yes, Miss Beeler. I can't remember — no one ever does — but I was told that I cried on my first day of school. They had to get my brother out of his second-grade room, up the hallway, to calm me down. I think a lot of kids cried that first day. We little five-year-old darlings — or monsters, depending on a parent's (or a neighbor's) point of view — had to leave the comfort of our backyards all over south Minneapolis that day in September 1944. We entered other schools with names like Bancroft, Minnehaha and Keewaydin. We probably had to share the toys my brother told me were hidden in big wooden boxes against a wall.

I remember vividly my first day of school, while the rest of it is more or less blank. My mother took me to Bancroft Elementary School, which was maybe four blocks from home. My older brother was starting the second grade, but that had no resonance for me, a four-year-old (who turned five later in the month). What stood out was, as I was sitting crying with my mother, the teacher came over to me and said, "If you don't stop crying you'll get slapped." I immediately stopped wailing and never cried in school again.

RONALD PETERSON

Kindergarten was fun — half-day mornings, and Miss Kittleson was an older, sweet, gray-haired lady. The one thing I remember is that I loved the taste of paste. No crying there either and I loved that each of us had to bring our own rug to school for nap time.

ARLOINE HULLAR

Did I cry the first day of school? Heck yeah. My first school was Blaine Elementary. It was about a block away from Washington and Plymouth avenues, in north Minneapolis. It was just far enough away from our tenement that I had never been there before school started. So, I cried! First because I did not want to leave my familiar home and go to school. Second because, when I looked around at the kids I would be in class with [blacks, Hispanics], I realized that this blond, blue-eyed Norwegian kid was in for some thumping by the larger, older toughies who came from a couple blocks away. And I was right. Heck yeah, I cried!

CHARLES GUDMUNSON

My friend Connie and I were inseparable at age five and could hardly wait to go off to Bancroft together. Imagine our surprise when we got there, only to discover we were in separate classrooms — she in Miss Weatherby's and me in Miss Jacobson's. End of the world! Somehow our mothers must have intervened, and we ended up together as we did for the next six years.

JOANNE MAHRE

My mother told me to follow the creek home. After class that first day I came to a corner and started to cry because I couldn't remember which direction to take to "follow the creek" back home. A girl in my class saw me crying, came up to me and told me which direction to go. I was so ashamed and embarrassed by that episode that I never spoke to the girl the rest of that school year at Minnehaha.

RONALD EIKAAS

The boys cried more than the girls did. Girls didn't have time for tears. It took a few years and a few grades for me to find out why. The "little princesses" were already currying favor with teachers, starting with Miss Beeler that day — offering to separate the construction paper and crayons by colors and bringing out nap mats from the cloakroom. Fine! The boys were concerned about learning.

> My great friend [Gordy Seashore] showed me how to draw an apple tree in kindergarten. We were very poor, and I don't recall eating an apple until I was in sixth grade! No one in our neighborhood had an apple tree, so how was I expected to draw an apple tree, having never seen one? This is how I passed all my grades [copying from the person next to me].
>
> GREGORY LARSON

We looked up the hallway toward the other classrooms then back at Mr. Swenson. He repeated that it was OK as long as we stayed in our stockinged feet and on the newspaper.

Two classrooms up. I had begun to catch onto things in second grade and was pretty good at those "animated flip books" that made it look like the people in the snapshots were actually moving. Magic!

I stared through the glass panes of the door of my third-grade room. Empty now, of course. My desk was over against the window. I could look out and see the playground and my house across the street.

Two things happened when I used to sit there. They were both about loss — one big, one small.

A boy, two desks back of me, was absent a lot. One day Miss Horkey told us that he was very sick and wouldn't be able to come back that year. She had us put together a scrapbook of pictures that we had cut out from magazines from home, happy scenes that we pasted into the book. His mom came by to pick up our present one day. She cried as she thanked us. Not long after, we heard that our schoolmate had died. The room was quiet for the rest of the day.

I didn't think that kids died that way — not by drowning over at Lake Nokomis or being hit by a car down on River Road — but in a hospital, or home in a bed. I knew that old people, like our grandparents, had bodies that simply wore out and died. Those were "good deaths," and they got their names in the paper, many for the first time. But why kids? Why "bad deaths"?

The other loss happened when one of my best friends, Jerry — I had three that year — came up to me on the playground to say good-bye. He was moving to Iowa because his dad was being transferred. I couldn't believe it. I didn't think kids moved out of our neighborhood. It was such a nice place to grow up in.

Bobby and I passed the library. Books. My mom wanted me to read the books on the shelves of Longfellow Library, across from Minnehaha Park. The words never stuck. I can remember the brightly polished wooden floors and a nice lady sitting behind a front desk. I only went with my mom because of the promise of a stop on the way home at the Dairy Queen.

Third-grade girls at Hiawatha: **Front row:** *Bonnie Rundell, Charlene Schermerhorn.* **Back row:** *Darlene Sjosted, Lorraine Larson, Gwendolyn Holloway, Judy Johnson, Jane Hagen, Naomi Curtis. Courtesy Jane (Hagen) Hess.*

I loved to read and looked forward to the bookmobile that came every other week. I was only allowed to check out eight books. Never enough for two weeks. My goal was to read every book in the bookmobile. I finally realized they kept changing them.

JORUN OLSON

I remember my mom sitting down with me in the living room, along with a small easel chalkboard and chalk, and going over the alphabet and words with me. I remember not paying attention once and getting slapped for it. I was maybe three, and my mother was a great proponent of books and libraries. The first book I remember owning was about pirates, and I loved it dearly.

RONALD PETERSON

At Howe we had an "extra" classroom set aside as a "branch" of the Minneapolis Public Library. Two librarians were there for one or two days a week. Each class would have an assigned time to go to the library as a group once a week. I loved books and looked forward to this opportunity. In the early grades I particularly enjoyed Maud Hart Lovelace's *Betsy-Tacy and Tib* series, The summer after fourth grade, I spent the whole summer in bed. I was suffering from rheumatic fever. I read books all summer long. Reading got me through that ordeal. Even now it would be difficult for me to imagine a good life without books to read.

CYNTHIA KERSTEN

I loved going to Longfellow Library. When my brother got his license, he took me there to get my library card — in those days a precious thing. Mom didn't drive so I rode my bike there during the summer. I loved the *Betsy-Tacy and Tib* series and couldn't wait to read the next one. I also read all the Nancy Drew books. I loved the library building itself. I can still see it, inside and out, in my mind. In my young mind, it was magnificent.

CAROL PETERSON

We moved to 45th Avenue and 45th Street when I was six. My sister Jan (RHS '55) and I walked many, many times to the library (Longfellow) to get our *Betsy-Tacy and Tib* books (Maud Hart Lovelace). We each had a nickel for the Dairy Queen for our trip home loaded with books. Imagine a walk for a six- and an eight-year-old in that neighborhood today. Many summer hours reading, until our mom asked for help: "Are you girls still reading up there?" This from a woman who taught first grade until she was 67. She, a voracious reader herself, started teaching when I started first grade.

CAROL THORSON

Then up to the front part of the building — the principal's office, his secretary's station and the nurse's office. I remembered the day we were taught the difference between the words "principal" and "principle." The teacher said that our principal, then Miss Carlton, was our "pal."

Looking back now, she could've been a "Mrs.," but we didn't think principals had husbands or kids — or did stuff outside of school. All I remember now were her big eyes, magnified behind eyeglass lenses with wire frames, the kind the nuns wore at St. Helena's in Sunday-school classes.

We walked around the hallway to the upper grades.

In addition to long division, decimals and geography, in fourth grade we also learned the value of saving money. That lesson never stuck with me.

I'm wondering if all of us, regardless of which grade school we went to, enjoyed the convenience of being able to put money into our Farmers and Mechanics savings account at school. My memory is, the opportunity was available every Thursday. There was a little envelope you filled out, and you included your bank book. I tried to bank 25 cents every week. I believe the bank books were returned on Mondays. When I left for college my account had $500 in it.

CYNTHIA KERSTEN

I peeked into the gym and remembered the assemblies. And the songs we had to rehearse for them.

In fourth grade, Mrs. Warmbold used a pitch pipe she held up to her mouth — loose skin under her arms jiggling and flapping like a chicken's neck — to make sure we all started out on the same note when we sang "America the Beautiful" and "Faith of our Fathers." On the times when we got it right — seldom — she smiled as if we were the pitch-perfect Mormon Tabernacle Choir.

Mrs. Dahl next door, the other fourth-grade teacher, might not have agreed with her.

The lessons became more frequent the closer we got to the Christmas pageant. The sixth-graders showed off with an audience-pleasing "Joy to the World" as they paraded into the gymnasium. Miss Beeler's little kindergarten darlings struggled through "Away in a Manger."

Every Memorial Day, the whole place smelled of spring flowers — up on the stage, down on the floor where we would gather. And half way through the ceremony, every year, the same teacher would start crying and run out of the gym. Her brother had been killed in the war that had ended a few years earlier.

I remember the time I played *Cielito Lindo* and *Ciribiribin* on my clarinet and Arloine Dolan accompanied me on the piano at a recital. As my book-reading career never took hold, neither did my musical one.

Ah! Fourth grade. Spelling exercises. I found it hard to spell the name of the big river of our childhood. It got bigger as it flowed on its way down south, and people wrote books and sang songs about it. It was just three blocks and one patch of woods from our school. Our teacher made us stand beside our desks and spell it out, all together as one group: "M-I-S-S-I-S-S…" But that was easier than standing alone at the blackboard in front of the class. We could skip a few letters, being in a row of desks with other classmates. It was the same with words when we recited the Pledge of Allegiance or sang "God Bless America." I mouthed a few I didn't know, holding back a giggle while I sneaked a peek two rows over at Butch Born who giggled back at me while mouthing his own guesses.

This was about the time the girls got their reward for sitting straight at their desks and smiling through all the lower grades. Untouchables. They could do no wrong. They had been quietly scheming their way as they moved up the hallway and around the corner to the higher grades. By the time they got to Mrs. Dahl's or Mrs. Warnbold's side of the building they were teachers' pets — always first with their hands up. The boys raised theirs, maybe seconds later. The teachers never asked them if they had the same answers as the girls. Maybe they didn't, but wouldn't admit it.

But, sometimes, the boys got their revenge.

> Mrs. Dahl, fourth grade, asked who Will Rogers was. I waved my hand immediately and said, "Roy Roger's dad." Everyone howled.
>
> CAROL THORSON

The boys had to stay back and clap the chalk dust out of the erasers when they were disobedient, or write over and over that they would not do something they'd been caught doing. What about the girls? What if they had brought a frog into the classroom or stuck their used Juicy Fruit under the desk top or pulled at Naomi's braids? It was all so unfair.

Butch came up to me at recess one day and told me that the girls got the soft treatment because, "all our teachers were girls once." Why didn't I think of that?

> One morning I was told by my teacher to go to Principal Jasperson's office. What kind of trouble could this mean? After being seated she asked me if I was on the school grounds last night. I confessed that I had been there. She went on to scold me for swinging on the flagpole. Apparently, this was a rather grievous offence. My first crush and a few others took turns hanging on to an untethered rope from the flagpole and catapulting from a low wall to

swing in full circles around the pole. Having been chastised by an adult other than my parents, I wondered if I was a troublemaker.

PAUL WULKAN

Gloria [Blumke] lived across the street from Minnehaha. I was in grade school, and … Gloria sat in front of me with long, curly dark hair that fell on my desk. I remember fighting the temptation to dip a few strands into the ink well.

RONALD EIKAAS

While I knew that the girls had better handwriting skills, on one awards day at Hiawatha I found myself standing up at the blackboard with them. An important woman from downtown had come by our south Minneapolis school to hand out Palmer Method certificates for superior penmanship. I told my mom when I got home that day that I got an award from a "Mrs. Palmer" who had visited our school.

Some sad days were mixed with happy ones. One Valentine's Day Mrs. Warmbold stood at the front of the room next to a big cardboard box. She pulled cards out, calling out boys and girls whose names were on the cards. We walked up to the front of the room and took them back to our desks. One kid got just one or two of them from his fellow classmates. I peeked over at him. He was looking down at his folded hands on the desktop. He stayed inside that recess.

We went up the hallway to an open door of one of the narrow supply closets. I looked in — rather, I smelled in. And there it was. The musty smell coming from the shelves of stacked white writing tablets — more rag than paper — next to cartons of No. 2 pencils. It was an assault on one's sense of smell when you ran your nose down and across the top sheet. When you rubbed your finger tips over the paper, it felt like the fine-grade sandpaper your dad used in his workshop.

It would be the second "smell memory" that I would take away from grade school. The first one had happened back on the other side of the building — the sweet smell of grade-school paste — that shiny, sticky goo in the big jars. It was a kid's delight to lick the custard off a dipped-in finger.

Fifth grade was the scene of the dreaded spelling bees. Carol Peterson always bested me in those contests. Seems I was often the last boy standing at the blackboard, she the last girl. When I'd get tripped up on words like "equator" and "discourage" — she'd become the winner.

I'm still smarting from those defeats. I remember staring up at the ceiling, hoping for some sort of divine inspiration and guidance, only to have Mrs. Gruver interrupt my prayer by saying, "Henry, your time is up. Please take your seat."

Carol lived on the other side of the Hiawatha playground. When I was playing cub football on the field late into those autumn evenings under park lights, I'd see her upstairs light on. I knew she was practicing for upcoming spelling competitions. Fine, but we boys had to master single-wing running plays for Coach Armstrong.

A few of us won the much-envied positions of patrol boy and girl in the fifth grade. I began my tour of duty with the new red flags on wooden poles with a bright yellow "STOP" printed on it. The year before, they still had the metal hand-held signs, yellow with black trim, the kind you could use to slice your initials into a tree — if you were good at it.

I assumed my post right across the street from my house.

With that flag I had a power I'd never held before. Once — maybe the devil made me do it — I dropped it down in front of an oncoming car when no kids were around to cross the street. The car stopped. Its driver got mad at me. I looked away as I quickly jerked the flag back up. Had he jumped out of the car and come over, I'd have dropped the flag and run across the street to my house. Maybe to hide. That episode went unnoticed and unpunished. The next one did not.

I snapped the wooden pole while trying to vault down the sidewalk with it on my way back to the school building. I was sent directly to the principal's office, and Ms. Carlton relieved me of my duties — cashiered from the force — on the spot. No recourse. We were not unionized. I took off the coveted white belt and handed it to her secretary.

But she gave me no note to take home. She sensed the shame was enough. I also think she had gotten to know my mom and dad from the PTA meetings and didn't want to upset them. Now, that was a real "pal." I only lived across the street from the school, but it was a long walk home that day. Dishonorably discharged.

Then it was on to the last of our grade-school career. A few sixth graders elsewhere had mastered correct spelling and moved on to other challenges.

Jeanett Pfeifer (Corcoran Elementary School, 1951) was the object of their poetry.

"When you get married and live in France send me a pair of your old man's pants."

CHUCK GUDMUNSON

"Roses are red, violets are blue, God made us all but who made you?"

JANEL SCRIVEN

"Roses are red, violets blue, some like you belong in the zoo. P.S. I love you."

LANNY SMITH

We continued with split classes. Mrs. Wyoma Bunn was the other sixth-grade teacher.

Wyoma Bunn had to comfort me cuz I didn't get in Arloine, Jane, or Carol Pete's sixth-grade class. I went out carrying my safety-patrol flag, crying, and some kid said, "Did you flunk?"

CAROL THORSON

Mrs. Norberg was my fifth grade teacher at John Ericcson. She was very nice, not too strict, and close to retirement. I thought she was a good teacher until I got to sixth grade. My sixth-grade teacher, Mrs. Alexander, had the reputation of being strict and demanding. We were supposed to know fractions and a few other things by the time we reached her class. Well, we were never taught fractions in fifth grade, so Mrs. Alexander had to double up on the math portion of her class, plus a few other subjects. I had to work hard in sixth grade.

PAUL GORGOS

Bobby and I walked up to Mrs. Gruver's classroom and looked at the empty desks where we'd been sitting but a week earlier, on Ribbon Day. I smiled and looked out to the side yard and thought of Mr. Swenson's remark. Yes, we'd had our arms around our girlfriends, and a classmate was taking snapshots with her Brownie camera.

We went back around the hallway in our socks, put our shoes on and left through an open door.

Author, Graduation Day, Hiawatha Elementary School, June 1951.
Courtesy Carolann (Hendrix) Lavell.

Graduation Day, Hiawatha Elementary School, June 1951.
Front row: *David Twaites, Larry Grady, Henry Gallagher, Janice Erickson, Joan Larson, Jim Dykstra, John Pollard, Jack Born.* **Second row:** *Kent Sherwood, Arloine Dolan, Carol Peterson, Jane Hagen, Joanne Johnson, Valerie Harrington, Doug Nash.* **Back row:** *Arnold Sandin, Donald Johnson (head). Courtesy Carolann (Hendrix) Lavell.*

2

We were lucky at our grade school. There it was, a whole city block of park-board property right across the sidewalk where we spent our recesses. Keewaydin School had such a next-door "neighbor" as well.

> My favorite class time at Keewaydin was lunch, because we got to go home for lunch for an hour and a half. We would race home, eat in ten minutes, and be back to the park to play softball for an hour or more. Other times we would play marbles with shooters, steelies and agates — a big bag of marbles each day — Jon Engfer always beat me back to the park. In the spring we played with our yo-yos, doing "walk the dog," "around the world" and various other tricks.
>
> DOUGLAS LARSON

Others didn't have it so nice.

> I didn't care much for recess [at Wenonah] on the dusty gravel playground. Only two swings, a teeter-totter and monkey bars. Or you could sit on the gravel and play marbles. Not so fun for us girls, who were required to wear dresses — no jeans or long pants.
>
> JORUN OLSON

[Although we didn't have a city playground next to our school, like Hiawatha or Keewaydin did] recess was a great time for us [at Howe]. We didn't have any playground equipment, but we enjoyed playing games such as Rover Red Rover send (name of kid) right over, tag and just running around. My classmate Tom Dahlin pushed me down while we were playing, and I broke my left arm. I am left handed so got out of a few spelling tests.

PAT EIDE

Grade-school recess, Hiawatha.
Front row: *Tom Tanner, Roland Meyers, Henry Gallagher, Jack Born, (unknown), Oscar Blegen, Larry Grady.* **Second row:** *Bruce McKusick, Glen Newman, Jim Meyers, Donald Johnson, (unknown), Arnold Sandin (unknown), Jack Holmgren.* **Back row:** *(unknown).*

I looked out across the dirt field and remembered back a few months ago when the surface of the ice rink was more puddles than ice. That's when the city's Park Board came out and dismantled the warming house and stacked it up at some warehouse until another skating season. In a week or so, they'll send out the "box" and two volunteers from the U (University of Minnesota), and our summer will officially start.

The huge wooden box contained a delight of games and sports gear designed to while away kids' summer hours (even if some no longer wanted to be called "kids"): ring toss games, bean bags, "cannycan" pins, on up to softball and volley ball equipment.

Some of us found recreation outside the box — mumbley-peg with a jackknife, for instance. We'd try to flip a knife from various positions on our body so the blade would stick into the ground. If you got through all the steps successfully and your opponent failed to reach that mark, a winner was declared and got to punch a wooden peg into the ground. The loser had to pull it out with his teeth. Arloine watched us one day and walked away at the peg-pulling stage: "Oh! That's yucky!"

Other neighborhoods had different versions of the game.

> Carol Hanson lived on 30th Avenue, third house from the corner. I spent nearly every day there in the summer between sixth and seventh grade. (I was not from a typical household.) No one was ever home at my house. We played mumbley-peg. Whoever got closest to the other person's foot when you threw the knife won the game. I ended up stabbing her in the foot. Blood. She ran into her house. It was the end of a good relationship.
>
> DOUG LARSON

We headed back across the playground toward my house. My dad had built a screened-in back porch. He and my mom sat there summer evenings, reading. My brother and I sat there summer afternoons, gambling. This was well after the kiddie card games that we had played inside on the living-room floor — Old Maid and Go to the Dump. We were now playing man games — five-card draw, stud and black jack. Some of the guys lipped their cigarettes when they dealt the cards while listening to the Game of the Day. It was played on the tiny Admiral in between commercials for the Gillette safety-razor company. At times we also tuned in Mel Allen, the "The Voice of the Yankees."

My house was available for casino action. We played black jack and poker, starting as soon as school was over and often lasting into the early evening. We would have from four to seven guys playing every night. We usually warmed up for these activities by flipping coins at school, in between nearly every class period, often carrying the activity into the classroom when we could. It's funny, but gambling season only took place in the spring and ended as soon as we could get outside for baseball.

DOUGLAS LARSON

PART II

1

"Never miss an opportunity to go through a Minneapolis alley. The suburbs do not have them. Too bad."
TERRY FRUTH, a Minneapolis lawyer

"Just take a drag on it. C'mon, Henry."

"How do I — "

"Just breathe in the smoke — like sucking pop through a straw — hold it a few seconds and blow it out."

We were in the alley behind 44th, and I took a puff on a Lucky Strike. Dickie Hansen had lit it for me. Maybe I was thirteen. I gagged and coughed my way over to the side of Merlin White's garage. Leaned up against it. It was my first cigarette — my first vice. But what the heck… I knew the path to manhood would be rough at times.

> I always wanted a buzz cut or "heinie," but Clarence [the barber] would never give me one without my parents' permission. I finally went to a different barber at 38th and Chicago Avenue to get one without permission. This was another big step, on becoming an adult.
>
> PAUL WULKAN

Alleys — simple strips of pavement that ran behind our houses — designed for cars, junk, trash and garbage removal, and cats. But their inventors were not aware of a higher purpose — makers of boys-into-men.

Pity the kids today. They don't have alleys to walk down anymore. A lot of the moms and dads live in suburbs — on bent streets — boulevards, drives or lanes. Some even live on cul de sacs, something we thought French people did in privacy. Their kids on the first day of vacation might bang out through screen doors into a backyard and find themselves fenced in. No alley. No "Bobby" running down to meet him.

Their streets twist through neighborhoods with names like Evergreen Knoll, Goldenrod Lane, or Timber Wolf Circle. The garages have crept up to the front of lots, where they cling to the sides of houses rather than remain at the rear of the lot — where they belong — off an alley. There, residents could hide rusting tools, half-filled motor oil cans, old tires and — as some parents might've wished — disobedient children. And big front lawns that flow down to curbs. No sidewalks, where kids can ride their Radio Flyer wagons and tricycles and kill ants that dare cross their path, then move on to roller skates and bicycles.

One of the earliest memories I have from my alley — the garbage truck driver. I would run halfway up the alley to meet him. He was my friend. He would let me sit up in the truck and ride back down to our house at the edge of the alley. He was one of the first grownup persons I knew who was not a relative. I think that was before I met Ms. Beeler, my kindergarten teacher.

A few years later, as I and my buddies walked down alleys, the scenes were chaotic — overflowing garbage cans, scuffed backyards, left-out (or abandoned) toys, dented cars, an empty whiskey bottle up against a garage, kitchen garbage, and spilled gasoline. We came across noises and voices from backyards — dogs fighting dogs, brothers fighting brothers, a boat owner testing his Evinrude in a water-filled oil drum, grown-ups arguing and laughing behind dark-screened back porches, small-kid voices, too. "I'll trade you my *Blackhawk* for two of your *Batman*."

Some of the scenes were mysterious to our young eyes. Once, we came across what looked like a flattened balloon, a white one, lying on the ground. We thought it was left over from some kid's backyard birthday party.

Tommy said, "I know what it is, and it's not a party balloon."

I asked, "What is it, smarty-pants?"

"Well, if you guys don't know," he shot back, strutting a bit, "I'm not gonna tell you." He always ended with that smug answer — the quickest way we knew that he didn't know. (I would find out what a condom was a few years later when I saw some more of the "balloons" down by the river).

It reminds me of another time, walking back to our houses from Carol Peterson's under the Hiawatha playground lights. I asked Pollard what a "French kiss" was. He, too, smirked and answered, "Well, if you don't know, I'm not going to tell you."

We talked about our grown-up plans while going down alleys — big dreams of little boys. We didn't think girls had big dreams — or should have them. We didn't think that was allowed.

Girls did not have big dreams. It was not in our realm of possibility. I can remember walking home from Roosevelt and noticing a "House for Sale" sign with a female agent. I spent some real time thinking through the idea of a woman Realtor being competent. I finally decided that I would prefer one. We had altar boys at church. No altar girls or acolytes. Unheard of! That stuck in my craw.

RUTH JOHNSON

The alleys echoed with kid talk, "Can you borrow me a dime?" "You wanna come with?" "Don't be a scaredy-cat," "I see London, I see France, I see…"

We thought that other phrases were just as harmless, knowing little about racial slights. When a kid bought something from another kid, a set of comic books, a used yo-yo or fielder's mitt, we heard the comment "Did you Jew him down?" The highest seats at the auditorium down on 11th were called "nigger heaven." And picking someone in a game of tag or for sides over on the playground we sang out the nursery rhyme, "Eeny meeny miny moe, catch a nigger by the toe," not even knowing that in the original version, it was a tiger's toe that one had to catch, and clearly not knowing the racist implication of the word we used.

A few years later, we would hear about "fairies," "queers" and "fruits." Kid-meanness came both knowingly and unknowingly.

We had learning moments in alleys: how to spit through our teeth and lip-whistle. Then there were swear words to memorize, the ones that went beyond "darn" and "dang." One day I heard a big kid yell one out on the playground. I practiced saying it to myself on the way home that day. I tried it out on my brother. I thought it would be a neat thing to say.

It was the summer after our parents had taught us tennis on the courts across the street. After one game, my brother and I argued over who would take down the net. I called him that word. My mom heard it come sailing through our open screen windows — a son shouting a curse word at another son. Neither I nor my brother knew what it meant. She knew. One of her sons was being called a "bastard," by the other one. And called it not once, but, "Johnnie is a…" over and over again.

She wasted little time rushing from the dining room, through the kitchen and out the back door into our yard. She told my brother to take down the net. Once I got near her she grabbed me by the ear. Uh-oh! I thought, here comes that "hold-your-hands-out-palms-up" spanking with the little wooden ruler with the metal liner. It was stored in a kitchen drawer.

She whisked me through the kitchen — ignoring that drawer — and directly into the bathroom. She held my head, face down, over the sink. Rather than put the family brand tooth powder — Dr. Lyons — on a brush, she used Ivory soap to scrub the bad word out of me.

At Sunday school a few years earlier, we'd learned about guardian angels. They would always follow us around to keep us out of trouble. I don't know where mine was that day.

We had secret hiding places off the alleys. John Pollard would call my Drexel 3319 from his Parker 2495. (I don't think

I knew any other Drexel people then. Years later, Joanne Haugen told me she was one.) My mom would hand me the clunk-heavy telephone that sat on the little table in the dining room next to the Venetians. John was calling about meeting at our secret rendezvous under the eaves of the roof on Carlson's garage, down the alley. We went there to plot things.

I didn't use the phone very often, except to call John or Bobby. Or the times my mom called her sisters and turned it over to me to thank them for the Christmas and birthday gifts. But I did use it once to listen in on the "party line" we had with the Johnsons across the alley. I'd carefully pick up the receiver with my left hand, slowly release the button with a right-hand finger — and listen in. One time I heard an angry voice, "Is that you Henry Gallagher?" Mrs. Johnson told my Mom. I didn't do it anymore.

I don't know if girls had secret alley places where they'd meet. But I was pretty sure that they were not real "alley" people. Sidewalks out front were for "sugar and spice" girls. But there were exceptions.

We had a fun alley right outside our back door. It had a hill right in the middle of the block. Yes, an alley hill! Not a gradual incline but a hill! We went down it sledding and cardboarding in the winter, and biking in the summer. My sister and I raced each other to the bottom, often crashing into a concrete retaining wall. The alley was more like an extended playground for us. Hide and Seek after supper, running across it without having to look both ways. (Most people only had one car, which usually left early in the morning and didn't return until nearly suppertime.)

JORUN OLSON

The day a friend and I were out selling pieces of concrete, we walked the alley while neighbors were in their back-yards, working. Back doors were used more than front doors. I seldom walked on the front sidewalk.

ARLOINE HULLAR

But usually, girls stayed on the sidewalks out front. They skipped rope, giggling and whispering secrets to each other in that conspiratorial way that was the birthright of eleven- and twelve-year-old girls. I doubt if they told dirty stories, practiced swear words or learned how to inhale a Lucky or a Camel. May-be they talked about boys, as we did girls. But the talk, on both sides, remained just that, talk. At least for a few more years — until we discovered each other.

Often, if we saw girls in the alley we'd ignore them as they passed, maybe say some smart-ass thing, or chase them out of the alley. They'd go laughing and screaming through side yards, between houses, to get back out onto a front sidewalk — where they belonged.

When we were not plotting adventures or deep into "boy talk," we played alley and yard games. This went on throughout the day and continued after supper, until the streetlights came on. Sometimes we'd let one or two girls play, especially if they were good at boy things. It was OK if they ran like a girl but could throw a ball or a can like a boy.

> I played kick the can with the boys. The alleys were for things like running up and down with Fourth of July sparklers. Boys and girls roller-skated down the sidewalks. I was definitely a klutz at softball. But I was a very good runner, and good at kick the can. I was not a tomboy, I think, but learned to play with boys.
>
> RUTH JOHNSON

Besides kick the can, draw the frying pan and other hide-and-seek adventures, we were into cops and robbers, and cowboys and Indians. We had an arsenal of rubber-band guns, cap pistols and pea shooters — and an occasional slingshot.

> Alleys were our life's highway to many experiences and destinations during those early years. They were the fastest route to my friend's house, to the drugstore, to Ring's hobby shop, the local grocery store, Pete's barber-shop, and Paradise Bakery. We played kick the can, hitting tennis balls off the side of Peterson's garage, and saw how far a slingshot could go — till we broke Rosendahl's window, four houses up. (His son snitched on us to his dad.) And we rode a Doodlebug through the alley, although we were too young to do so.
>
> JOSEPH STEINER

When we wanted to hang out with our friends, we set up our own play dates. We ran over to their house, stood on their sidewalk or near their bedroom window and literally "called" for them until they either came out or their mother came out and told us to stop yelling and go home.

JORUN OLSON

Alleys were all-purpose venues.

Who was that cute, curly-haired blond girl all the boys tried to impress? We both right away said, "Judy Westlund." Used to ride our bikes through the alley to see if she was in her backyard and try to get her to notice us.

JOE STEINER

A bicycle wasn't the only thing he rode.

[It was during] the Aquatennial week in 1947, with the famous day and torchlight parade. I was the envy of my neighborhood, because my dad worked for Rothschild department store, which had a float in the parade. So they needed an eight-year-old boy and girl to ride on the float dressed in Dutch outfits with wooden klompen shoes [Dutch clogs]. The float was decorated in tulips. I got to be the shy boy riding on that float in the aquatennial parade. That helped my status in the neighborhood.

JOE STEINER

In our early years, we were not age conscious. We'd let anyone play with us. Later, when we grew up and reached sixth grade, we ran with our own. We'd never be seen going down the street or an alley with a kid a lot younger than us — unless a mom made one of us look after a tagalong younger brother or sister. When we were in fifth grade, no kid in seventh wanted to be seen playing with us. That was the rule, hard and fast.

The alley games were only interrupted when a car, or sometimes a Harley or a Cushman scooter, even a Doodlebug, turned into the alley. The junk man, too. You knew when Wayne's older brother came through with the broken muffler on his Chevy. The mothers in kitchen windows would moan, "When will Marion's kid ever fix that…?"

We also stepped aside a few times when a kid came by with a new birthday bicycle — no doubt already stripped down, a mitt hanging from its handlebars. Some of them had baseball cards taped to the frame. The chatter in the spokes sounded like a motorbike.

One time we stopped playing when a kid called out from a neighbor's backyard garden, "Hurry up, I got a garter snake that's gonna throw up a frog it just ate." We ran over. A girl who was playing with us hung back by the garage. The kid was holding the snake down with a broken tree branch. It was slowly pushing something in its belly closer to its mouth. Then the snake lost interest and stopped. So did we and went back out to the alley and down to another yard.

One had an apple tree. Green ones waiting to be picked. We pulled off the picks with military precision. We stationed a look-out at the edge of the alley to alert us if the owner of the house (and the tree) returned home unexpectedly. If he did, we'd scatter over a neighbor's fence or through a side yard out onto the street.

Three backyards up the alley, old man Bremmer had another apple tree, the best one on our block. Problem was, he was always home. We went on raids anyways,[3] salt shakers in our back pockets. With him, it was always the same thing. He waited till one of us was halfway up his tree before he shouted at us from his back porch. It was scary in the beginning — an angry voice through a darkened screen from an old man whose face we couldn't see. At first, we ran. After we found out he was all scare, we finished the heist and beat it back out to the alley, our pants pockets stuffed with apples.[4]

We never saw him out in front or down the street. My mom said his wife had died a few years earlier — then his dog. We were glad the trees were in yards near our houses so we could rush back to our bathrooms and throw up the sourness in our stomachs. The salt could only help so much.

---

[3] Out east my friends often catch me using the Minnesota alternate for "anyway."

[4] We stuffed the apples into the pockets of our "overalls," the jeans of our time. Ours were not really over "all," just waist high with hammer loops. Some of the dads on our block wore the real thing when they went off in the mornings to work in the mills and factories. No Levis yet. They were for the farm kids who came into the Twin Cities for the Minnesota State Fair. Not us. We were sophisticated. We were city.

Another favorite was Carlson's garden, where we dug up some rhubarb. Minutes later we were back out in the alley, biting on the salted stalks of the sour red and green root. Funny how we ate vegetables covered with dirt but not the ones put on our supper plate by our moms. One time I was biting into a rhubarb stalk when I felt a sting off my right elbow. I looked down and saw a large black rubber band lying at my feet. I turned quickly but the shooter had ducked back behind the garage.

We often went into a backyard of one of the kids (or a kid-tolerant neighbor) who lived in a house with a low roof line and played "Annie Annie Over." At times during the game, someone would yell out "pigtail." I had no clue what it meant. I had the same confusion in makeup football games over on the playground when someone on the other side would shout "PPOR" (put, pass or run) on fourth downs. We'd repeat that signal and nod back and forth at each other, acting as if we knew what it meant. I didn't. I thought, what else could they do with a football?

We got real thirsty on hot days. Even though I wasn't in my own backyard, I went over to a hose lying on the grass. Took a drink. Hot! Yuck! What a rubber taste.

> We were told not to drink water from the garden hose for fear of contracting polio.
>
> DAVID GILMAN

When the afternoon clouds darkened, we changed the location of our fun. At the first roll of thunder, we'd abandon the alley and yards, run home, jump into swimming suits and dash across the street to the tennis courts. We brought along rags to plug the drains. Then we'd lie down and splash around in the backed-up water that was slowly pooling across the two courts — rainwater warmed by the stove-hot concrete surface.

> We went swimming in the street when Sibley Park would flood after downpours.
>
> JOSEPH STEINER

At times, minor alley crimes went beyond green apple capers.

> For a while there, I was running around with some window-breaking guys.
>
> DOUGLAS LARSON

Occasionally, low-grade alley mischief went on at night. Kids a few years older than us went in search of free gasoline. There was always one in the group who was the bravest (or dumbest); he squatted and siphoned gasoline from a car parked in a driveway. The others acted as lookouts, staring at windows and the back doors of a house. The poor kid put his mouth on one end of a short rubber hose and put the other end into the car's gas tank. He sucked up the gasoline, pulling his mouth off at the last second (or almost the last) as he whipped the hose into a gallon can at his feet. Spit out whatever he had gagged on.

Sometimes bullies went beyond low-level alley mischief. While we may have been taught right from wrong by our parents, church, and teachers, we also learned lessons in the alleys — when bullies took them over as their domain, as if they "owned" them. They were usually a few school grades older than us and showed us the dark side of kid-life, visiting violence on their own kind by beating us up.

If we happened to be in the alley at those times, we kept our distance and stared, too scared to do anything else. You felt the danger in the pit of your stomach before it reached your head or your heart. They were not fights. They were beatings — up against the backsides of garages, where grown-ups couldn't see. Yet, some apron-wearing moms had magical powers. They could see around garage corners. Mrs. Bergdahl, a one-person neighborhood-watch team, would call out, "What's going on back there?" and "Tommy Erdahl, what are you doing out there?"

Maybe the tormentor had a grudge over some imagined slight by his victim. More often it was just a random opportunity for him to show off for a thug-mate. He might follow a kid into the alley and "pants" him because the kid wasn't "normal." In fact, the initiator might himself have been the not-normal one. He could've been a kid with the dark impulses of bipolar disorder or one conditioned to violence from a trauma-filled home. Maybe a parent had made life miserable for him. He'd witnessed his father's alcohol-driven abuse of his mother or, more immediate, suffered beatings himself. Some may even have been sexually molested by an adult. So, he took it out on others.

We did have bullies in the near neighborhood. When walking to Folwell we would pass by their house but walked on the other side of the street to be safe. They were brothers, nasty kids. But we did have an ace in our pocket because we had the Hastings living across the alley. The oldest was Jim (Butch) Hastings and he was big and tough. One time, one of my friends got too close to the brothers, and they were not nice to him. So a few days later, Butch happened upon them at Sibley Park and set things right. We were never bothered by them again.

JOSEPH STEINER

Terry [Baxter] was a good friend. We played park board football together while in junior high. I had a paper route and was out collecting monies from my route customers one evening at dusk, and this guy — I'd heard of him — came out of nowhere, picked me up and took my route book and tossed it around. Later, another guy was picking on my brother Bruce, and I stepped in and got him in an arm lock, his face down in the snow. For 15-20 minutes he wouldn't say "uncle," but finally, he said he'd had enough. He left, and that's when the rest of the bullies started to pick on me. I mentioned this to Terry the very next day. After that I was home free. No one ever picked on me again. That says a lot about Terry's power and the respect he had in junior high.

GREGORY LARSON

One time a grown-up neighbor came out into the alley to break up a bully beating that we had been watching from a distance. After the kid had run away, the man looked over at us and said, "None of them have good fathers."

We saw more than what the girls saw.

> I don't remember anyone getting beaten up in our neighborhood. That's more a guy thing. My brothers (nine and eleven years younger) could probably tell some stories about that.
>
> JORUN OLSON

It was odd (or not so) that the bullies often were sets of brothers — a culture of violence running through a single household. We had one such set of siblings living over near our blocks. One of them tormented a kid who couldn't fend for himself. They stuffed him into a metal trash bin on the Hiawatha playground, the cans with lids on the top and a slot in front. Each year they would go off to the Southside picnic at Powderhorn looking for fights. Years later, I heard that the brothers had come from an abusive household.

For a few of those summers, we had to abandon the alleys and yards as polio crept through the city (even the bullies had to stay home). My brother and I were on lock-down in our backyard, not even allowed to sneak messages to the outside world — that is, kids down the block. We later learned that they had to "shelter-in-place" as well.

If we crossed the street to the playground and breathed the air, we were told, we would catch the virus — that from the same mom who had warned us about the air around Sheltering Arms. If we drank water from the fountain over on 43rd — the one whose nozzle was always stuffed with broken Popsicle sticks — we'd get polio that very instant. No bubble-gum blowing either. Same mom, same reasoning.

Different families had different ground rules for their kids during the citywide scare.

My mom had polio during the epidemic. We were quarantined for two weeks. Bonnie Leppa and I used to play dress-up. We would throw shoes back and forth across the yards, because we each had to stay in our yard. I remember going to the Sister Kenny Institute and waving at my mom who was in the window waving at us kids. She was happy none of us got it.

JANE HAGEN

During the polio epidemic we could continue to play with our neighborhood gang. We had to stay on Isabel Avenue and could no longer go to Highland pool to swim as we had been doing each evening, with parents taking turns.

SUSAN CODUTI

It was a bizarre cautionary rule for one family in our neighborhood unless the city's health department had somehow certified that the cruel disease chased down kids on their streets but not down their alleys.

The "official" rule was, play only with kids on your own block. I lived on the west side of 47th Avenue, between 37th and 38th streets. The rule meant that I could play with friends across the alley but not friends across the street. Even as a child, that seemed arbitrary to me. I remember those phone calls my parents would get from friends who had taken their offspring to emergency rooms, only to discover it wasn't polio. I did, however, have a second cousin who contracted polio, and even became the Minnesota Poster Child.

CYNTHIA KERSTEN

… no lakes or pools, only garden hoses and sprinklers.

JOANNE MAHRE

For two years, when I was in the lower grades, we were forbidden to go to swimming pools, the lake, and crowded places. The epidemic closed schools, leading to the creation of the Minnesota School of the Air, a radio show aimed at homebound children. The State Fair was canceled in 1946 in order to slow the spread of the dreaded virus. Some adults got it as well as children, but too many children died or were paralyzed by the disease.

RUTH JOHNSON

The cars parked in the driveways on our blocks were Chevies, Plymouths and Fords. (Even though John Pollard's dad drove a Terraplane, and so did Joanne Mahre's.) An occasional Studebaker or Nash came down the alley — sometimes even a Mercury or a Buick. But if a Cadillac or a Packard appeared, it wasn't one of our neighbors. Maybe someone who'd come back to his old block to visit less well-off relatives. Those cars went down alleys in neighborhoods farther west, over by the lakes.

In the late '40s, the dads started to do trade-ins and buy-ups. It was a celebrated event on a Saturday morning when one came down the street in a just-bought car right from a Lake Street showroom. If his kids were in the backseat, they'd stop and let us come up to the open window to catch a whiff of the new-car smell. That aroma of newness in our 1949 Chevy was soon overpowered by the lingering odors of my dad's Camel cigarettes.

For kids, the Cushman scooter was the last step before a car.

I remember in ninth grade, one kid got a Cushman motor scooter and he was the envy of every boy, even though he was too young to have one. The closest thing we had in our neighborhood was a red Doodlebug.

JOE STEINER

Some started early.

My dad bought the new Doodlebug for me as an Xmas
present 1947, third grade, but couldn't take it out until
the snow was off the ground. Started it many times in the
garage. Mother wasn't happy about the gift.

RON EIKAAS

2

When we tired of the alley and the playground across the street, we jumped on our bicycles — next to the streetcar, the only other means of escape out of our neighborhood. A bicycle! Freedom! Girls! The wind in your face. The Far Horizons. Well, "far" being Lake Street and Minnehaha Falls.

Our parents bought my brother and me new Schwinns one summer. To my mom's dismay I stripped mine down to be accepted by my peers in the neighborhood. Who really needed a battery-powered horn and its casing along the top tube? And a head lamp? Overhead street lamps took care of that when you rode home at night. And who needed fenders, for that matter? The gradual strip-down by stealth took a week or two. I didn't want her to catch on right away.

One day, she looked out the kitchen window and saw the bare frame of a bike leaning up against our fence. She assumed that one of the kids on the block had come by. An hour later she caught on. It took some explaining to stop her from grounding me. I had to think quickly.

"But Mom, all the kids are beating me in the races on that side street down off River Road. Even that tomboy, Gary Nelson's sister. I needed to lighten the weight. Do you want your son to be neighborhood loser? Beat even by a girl, Mom? A girl?"

She relented. I don't think she believed all of my story. We both knew that Ellie Nelson was not inclined to compete with the boys in bike racing. But it wasn't a big lie, one that I had to go to confession about. Ellie did go down there to watch us race.

The first bike in our household was for my brother. A neighborhood boy (the late Bob Carlson, '57) came over to help in its assembly, since it was delivered unassembled in a paper box. Bicycles were the heart and soul of our childhood experience in Minneapolis, and I cannot remember when I first acquired one for myself. Our bike of choice was Schwinn, of course, which was the most popular. Columbia made bicycles as well, but they seemed clunkier. Advertising for both brands was found in comic books. There was one other, more exotic brand, Raleigh, but this was a funny-looking import. My first bike had a large basket to use for delivering newspapers and also a battery-powered horn, which, I think, I never used. Bikes, like their successors, cars, represented a milestone in development since they both were a totem of freedom. The latter were great with girls, but I wasn't mature enough to think of bikes being useful in the same regard.

RONALD PETERSON

We would ride our bikes, all while holding the fishing pole, tackle box and the worms. A favorite fishing place was a small hidden creek on the west side of the Lake Nokomis Bridge. We always caught a few sunfish, which we dutifully brought home for dinner. No matter what my mother had planned, she would still fry up my few fish as though I were a real contributor to dinner.

PAUL WULKAN

Bikes came with a single reflector on the back, but it broke off and was rarely replaced. Lights existed, but they were considered an extravagance used only by showoffs. For most kids, the entire concept of bike safety was reduced to a warning from their mother: "If you get run over, don't bother to come home for dinner." We rode our bikes (helmetless) down busy streets, zipping from one friend's house to another, never telling anyone where we were going next (as if we knew).

RUTH JOHNSON

Others felt the early sting of gender discrimination (read: boys first) in their families.

Walking was one of very few options for getting around. We only had one bike in our family, and usually someone else (read: one of my brothers) was using it.

JORUN OLSON

Mine was Columbia-blue and cream, complete with the ringing bell on the handlebar. Don't remember what age. Most fun was decorating them with many colors of crepe paper, weaving in and out of the wheel spokes, and riding them in our neighborhood parades.

JOANNE MAHRE

Some days we used our bikes to ride down to the Falls. We locked them across from the band box and went down the steps into the Deer Pen. We walked over to the creek and crossed the little bridge, then turned and went down along the path to where the Minnetonka-made stream slid into the Mississippi.

We used to take baseball bats down to the Deer Pen and whack at the carp that gathered in a little pool underneath the bridge that crossed the creek over to the path that ran down to the river.

JAMES C. MEYERS

Kids were fishing for sheepshead — worms hooked at the end of a long string weighted down with a rock. Over to the right was the outlet to a big sewer tunnel. Up to our left was dreaded Dead Man's Cave. The name had an exciting Huckleberry Finn connotation to it, just right for a boy's imagination. Legend held that if any kid ever tried to make it all the way to the back of the cave — on a dare or not — he would not only be late for supper, but would never make it back to the entrance alive.

Dead Man's Cave. We usually started our cave adventure by cruising down to Lake Street on our bikes to find a likely store to hit for cigarettes. We would send our best thief into the store. I never saw his methods but he was always able to procure a few packs of Lucky Strikes or Camels. (Even though no one inhaled, we liked our cigarettes strong in those days.) With our stash secured, we would head down to the Falls to Dead Man's Cave to puff away. After smoking for an hour or so we would crawl along the river banks or explore the creek and the falls.

DOUGLAS LARSON

I have great memories of the toboggan run going into the Deer Park at Minnehaha Falls. When I say great, I mean *terrifying!* It was long and winding, and had bumps in it that almost threw you off the toboggan. Of course, the walks on the paths from the Falls out to the river bring back wonderful memories — it was so beautiful and peaceful.

GLORIA BLUMKE

If my dad had a Sunday off from umpiring baseball, we would often go for a picnic to the Falls. My brother worked at the popcorn stand. Our St. Luke's Luther League had a cookout in the Deer Pen each year on a Friday night. Playing softball, campfire singing and roasting marshmallows were the sanctioned activities. Sneaking to climb behind the Falls was for those who were more daring and adventurous. Not sure what year Norway

Day began, but that too, was an annual event on a Sunday, beginning with a church service in the morning and going on all afternoon.[5]

JOANNE MAHRE

I guess I was in, about, the seventh grade. One Sunday afternoon, a kid from school rode to my house on his bike with his slightly older sister in tow. She wanted to go to the Falls and she was a sweet thing, so why not? We biked out there from my house near Folwell, crawled down under the falls, explored some of the trails, even looked into one of the caves. Then we headed for the Ford Bridge, parked our bikes near the top of the bluffs, and I proceeded to show this young lady my fearless climbing skills on the very steepest bluffs. I expect that I was quite pleased with my performance. Next thing I know, I'm waking up on our living room couch, at home, the entire family staring down at me, saying, "Oh, my God." There's blood on my Mom, and me, of course, blood on the policeman who carried me in. They're all saying, "We gotta go to General Hospital." Did I mention weeping? Oh yes, Mom, sister, neighbor ladies. I was plain

---

[5]After 80 years of separate celebrations of Norway Day and Svenskarnas Dag, the two latter-day immigrant populations in Minnesota got together to, in the words of the organizer, "bring the best of both and make an even bigger and better ethnic celebration for the Norwegians, Swedes and the Scandinavian community," now called "Scandinavian Summer Fest." (Norway House release, June 2015.)

whimpering, did not need tears. Apparently, I had tried one more spectacular climb, lost my footing and crashed, on my face, on a big rock about 30 feet down the bluff, and was knocked out, stone cold. The other kids ran to a house and told the lady what I'd done. She called the police, and they took me home. EVERY adult at my house had words of advice. Mom, Dad, cops, neighbors. Some said a few other things, too, like, "You damn well better not be riding that bike all over creation. And, "You better not go to the Falls, ever again." And, "Who do you think you are, anyway?" I was sewed up smartly by the GH intern, took a bunch of aspirin, moaned a lot, stayed home from school on Monday (only) and promised THE WORLD that I would never go to the Falls again. I did, of course, but not for a long time.

CHARLES GUDMUNSON

Minnehaha Falls was a hike for me, so our early experiences were often with our parents on picnics, etc. It was a large place, filled with mystery, and our adventure consisted of walking underneath the falls and often getting sprayed. Further toward the river lay the Deer Pen, Dead Man's Cave, etc.

RONALD PETERSON

There were two summer "festivals" (perhaps among others) on Sunday afternoons at the park—Swedish Day and Norwegian Day. I don't remember that my Swedish grandmother ever went, but my friend and I (Diane O'Dowd lived next door and was a year older than me) rode our bikes down to check out the activities. A roaming photographer from the Minneapolis *Tribune* spotted us, and thought that he had a good idea for a picture. He had Diane act as if she were reading from a Norwegian paper, while I sat beside her with a very puzzled expression on my face. The next day we were anxious to see if we had made the newspaper, but alas, we had not. I'm sure the editors had determined that they had images of that day that were better than our faked pose.

Cynthia Kersten

Bobby and I turned back and walked up the flat-stone steps that led to the Old Soldiers Home on the bluff overlooking the river. We were afraid to approach any of the old men because they were cranky and unfriendly, not like our grandfathers. While they smoked cigars and sunned themselves in long wicker bedlike chairs, we manned the cannon emplacement at the stone wall overlook. From there we defended south Minneapolis from enemy boats coming up the Mississippi.

We stayed up top on the bluffs and worked our way back around to our bicycles. At a break in the trees, I looked across the Pen at the ski jump — old and rickety-looking — its gray paint peeling in the bright sunshine. It looked like a huge playground slide nailed to stilts, all put together by an erector set. It looked so out of place on the grassy hill, as if the Park Board had forgotten one of the winter things that had to be taken down and put away until another season, the same way they did the warming houses.

If Minnehaha was *the* park in south Minneapolis, some kids farther away had one that was a close second.

> Powderhorn was such a gathering place and the center of so much activity in our neighborhood: South Side Picnic, Fourth of July, ice-skating (unique, with an island to skate around and a warming house for parties), pickup basketball games, horseshoes, playgrounds, picnic tables, etc.
>
> JOANNE MAHRE

> We were only three and a half blocks from Powderhorn Park. While we only went there on occasion, it was fun to skate around the island in the winter. But most special was the Fourth of July. Carnival-type rides were set up, all kinds of activities and races in the day hours and, at night, the fireworks. We would try to find a place on the hillside with a clear view of the sky. The fireworks were set off on the island. Because parking was difficult, we walked with our blankets and insect repellent. My cousins would come into the "Cities" from a farm. It was an adventure for them and a treat for us.
>
> PAUL WULKAN

Bobby and I hopped on our bikes and went home.

3

We also used up our summers going over to Lake Nokomis. For those of us who were not "up at the lake" or "down on the farm" families, it was another go-to destination (although there *was* a swimming hole at the creek behind Longfellow Library). The first few summers we biked over. Later we hitched rides, all too aware that soon-to-be men did not ride bikes

Dickie taught me to how to swim at Little Beach. That is, when he was not up to mischief. He would go under the water and suddenly pop up against (read: grope) the developing breasts of an unsuspecting girl, then plead, "Oh, sorry! Sorry!" At Big Beach, when he was not looking for cigarette butts outside the bathhouse he was peeking into the changing rooms on the girls' side.

Every neighborhood had at least one "Dickie." He was the one who stood out by getting into more trouble than all the other kids put together. He was a child of mischief, who caught the attention of all the moms who looked out their kitchen windows. And when he was not getting into garden-variety trouble, he was getting into accidents, the former often causing the latter. He was a low-grade menace — e.g., pulling the connector rod off the overhead electric wires at streetcar stops, falling off his bike in front of braking cars as he tried a look-no-hands showoff on slippery streetcar tracks, tearing shingles off a neighbor's doghouse. He was the first "accident waiting to happen" of my childhood.

One summer, Lake Nokomis meant two things to me: I had to learn how to swim and had to get a tan. All sons of Norway and Sweden on our blocks looked like Indians two weeks into summer vacation. I would become one of them. I was armed that first day. At Crane's, the day before, I insisted on buying a product that had to have either the words "Coppertone" or "Hawaiian" on the label, all the better if both words were on the plastic bottle. Before I lay down on the blanket I looked around. No one else had freckles or red hair. I would not be deterred. Down I went. Later that evening, writhing in pain, I used a small mirror to look in our big bathroom one. My back was the color of Spam.

> Summertime was spent at Lake Nokomis, and, living so close, we were there with everyone who was anybody, or so we thought. The big treat at the drugstore up the hill was ice cream cones, and of course at Big Beach it was popcorn and cotton candy.
>
> JUDITH KIBBY

> We biked over to Nokomis's Big Beach to see who had the guts to jump off the high-dive tower.
>
> JOSEPH STEINER

A few kids in our neighborhood went to Little Beach with no plans to swim. After learning the skills of shoplifting (and not being caught) down on Lake Street at Kresge's and Woolworth's, they migrated over to Nokomis. They had graduated to bigger heists, grabbing wallets and purses left on blankets by trusting owners who went into the water.

One day I went to Big Beach, and with Dickey's encouragement, I conquered the tower in a reckless, eyes-closed, fists-squeezed fall into the water. I never went back.

> I can't believe it now, but I did it. I jumped off the high tower at Big Beach at Lake Nokomis. I remember my friend Peggy Smith, a year younger than me. We slowly progressed, a step higher each day than the day before, until we got to the top. I think I walked back a few steps, looked around, went forward and jumped. I remember hitting the water and going down, down, until someone pulled me up by my hair. I think Peggy jumped one level down. The lifeguard scared us so bad we never dared go out there again. I think I was twelve, the summer before I entered Nokomis.
>
> JORUN OLSON

Others took on different things at Big Beach.

> After getting really sore from lifting weights at Dick Hume's [my paper route master] he asked me to join him at muscle beach at Lake Nokomis ... in the area where they have the parallel bar, rings and high bars. There were many RHS gymnastic members there. Dick tried to compete with these guys but could not, and I was a little

embarrassed for him until he went to the high bar. He jumped up grabbed the bar with both hands, then released his left hand and from a full hang he did two one-arm pull-ups, then grabbed the bar with his left arm and released the right arm and did another two one-arm pull-ups. I went home and told my dad what I had seen. The very next day he was looking in the want ads and saw one for a 160-pounds weight set for sale. He made a call, and we were on our way to buy the set the next weekend. He asked what else I needed. I said a bench and a squat and bench press. That weekend he built it and I was on my way.[6] Thanks, Dad.

GREGORY LARSON

---

[6]And for Greg, "on my way" included, among other things, playing professional football for the New York Giants for 13 years.

4

Back on our Hiawatha playground we played our baseball games with pick-up informality and abandon. If we played each other, we chose up sides the only way we knew. The two captains, often self-appointed, traded off gripping the bat hand-over-hand, each guy's fist alternating with the other guy's, moving up the bat. Whoever got the last grip at the top got to pick the first teammate for his side.

Our games with other teams down at Sibley or Longfellow were often played with the same kind of made-up-rules mentality. Sometimes we had a right fielder, sometimes we didn't. When we went on our bicycles on those road trips we often lost to better organized teams. Butch Born was our pitcher. He always seemed to pick a fight with the winning pitcher.

When we played the games at Hiawatha, Butch would show up with his ever tagalong retriever, Rex. The loyal dog would sit quietly alongside the edge of the field and watch his owner. Other dogs weren't so disciplined.

Not many guys in our gang had dogs, but my trusty pal was Blackie. He literally went everywhere with us. Unfortunately, sometimes he would end up in the wrong place and would be "arrested" by the dogcatcher. We had to bail him out of doggy jail three times, which was very expensive for our low-budget family. He also liked to watch our baseball games. The only problem with that was that he liked to chase me around the bases, biting at my pants leg whenever I got a hit, turning potential home runs into triples or less, and doubles into singles. I tried to break him of the habit, but nothing seemed to work. For big games, he had to stay home.

DOUGLAS LARSON

These baseball-playing days were in the last years before the Little League phenomenon took hold across the country. Formal rules and regulations. Well-intentioned parents not only showed up at games but moms called balls and strikes from the stands and angry dads followed umpires out to parking lots.

A few years later our ragtag baseball careers took a turn for the better. Dick and Jimmy Carlson introduced us to Harvey Peterson. He had lettered in baseball at Augsburg and, after college, had played on small-town leagues outside Minneapolis. Sponsors would pay their pitchers ten bucks just to show up, another ten if they won the game. The rest of the team members played for the love of the game and the trips to post-game beer joints out on the highway. Harvey entertained his team members at the player piano. Shortly after he agreed to be our coach, we found ourselves sitting on the grass at Longfellow Field, half naked, our bare legs splayed out in front of us, learning how to put on baseball pants over tucked-in stockings. I can't remember if we won many games that first season, but we sure looked the part.

By late August the up-at-the-lake kids had returned, their two weeks over as well as their romances with "townies." A few days before Labor Day, the park board box was taken away, our screened-in-poker porch closed for the season, and a mom ironed corduroys for the first school day.

When fall came, we played our football games with the same kind of casualness. Our teams were not as organized as programs in other neighborhoods — Keewaydin, for example, with the MFAC (Minnehaha Falls Athletic Club). We had Mr. Armstrong as our tackle-football coach, but we brought no trophies home. And when we played touch football, the kid who brought the ball doubled as the self-appointed quarterback and coach. He mapped out the plays with a Popsicle stick in the dirt.

Deeper into September, fall smells started drifting down and around our blocks. Neighbors burned leaves in wire containers and in curbside piles. Dead leaves that had escaped a fiery end were windblown up against garage walls, waiting for another gust to move them on to the side of the next garage, rattling on as they moved. The fallen apples in Bremmer's yard gave off a sickly-sweet smell of decay.

We threw an occasional football "down and long," the length of three garages, and kids forgot about kick the can. Not that we cared about the absence of the cans, but we were curious. A patriotic neighbor down the block had collected them for his kids to stomp flat onto his kitchen floor to "support the war." Seems that war support at home had outlasted the war abroad.

During World War II, we saved and recycled all metals, including the aluminum foil around sticks of gum. House-wives often sacrificed their aluminum cooking pots for the war effort — the metal was needed for airplanes. We saved soap shavings for laundry soap and collected scrap metal. We split gum wrappers, to separate the paper from the foil, which we collected for the war effort.

RUTH JOHNSON

October came and went with no promise, and we asked ourselves why we had to study certain subjects in school. Like history. Who needed it? Just a bunch of things happening, one thing after another.

The first sign of another skating season usually came in mid-November. From our dining room window, I would see Skip Swanson's dad out on the frozen dirt field, a half-chewed cigar in his mouth. He'd slowly zig-zag a huge fire hose in gloved hands back and forth across the ground. A steady stream of water gushed out of the hose that was hooked up to a hydrant down at the corner.

That's when I'd finally get to join my buddies on the ice with my new CCM speed skates. I'd found them under the tree the previous Christmas. My other two aunts had joined together to buy them. Aunt Ethel gave me flannel pajamas, once again, to add to the other two sets she had given me. Then there were the ceramic dogs. A few years earlier she had started giving me dog figurines for my birthdays. My brother got horses. I didn't know why she gave them to me. Toy soldiers would have been better. I could send them into combat from the edge of the living-room rug to fight Tojo's and Hitler's soldiers. Those bad soldiers gathered under the small table next to my dad's stuffed chair at the other side of the room.

But I couldn't send ceramic dogs into battle. They wouldn't take orders or hold a gun. Maybe they'd pee on my mom's rug. Each birthday the dogs kept coming as did the flannel pajamas each Christmas.

Our living-room floor. That's where my brother and I served in the war. I knew it was over one day when I was playing in the backyard and I heard a loud noise. My mom came running out the door to listen. The Minneapolis Moline horn was announcing to all of us in south Minneapolis that the war was over.

> My parents tried to keep news of World War II from me,
> but I remember the newspapers that they were always
> reading with intensity. Huge headlines — TOJO — in three-
> inch-high lettering; I had to figure out the code. My folks
> had perfected speaking in pig Latin, so I knew they were
> trying to hide something important from me. My grand-
> mother helped me break the code, revealing the sounds of
> the letters. So in 1944, I learned of the trouble we were in.
>
> RONALD EIKAAS

By the second "flooding" day, the Park Board would come out to put up the same warming house — board by board — that it taken down the previous spring. After Mr. Swanson had put down a final "glazing" of ice, he retreated to the warming house, threw some firewood into the pot-bellied stove and sat over in a corner with his girlie magazines. There, he would await the chaos of neighborhood kids who rushed out onto his annual masterpiece on ice to scar its sheen with their skate blades.

And rush onto it we did, once again, to open the skating season. It featured the usual excitement of pom-pom-pullaway, prisoner's base, mittens and choppers romances (which sometimes started with the boy grabbing the girl's woolen cap, a bizarre flirting ritual) and an occasional fight over on a snowbank — sometimes over a girl. The handlers for each of the skate-wearing combatants would agree in a prefight briefing that no fair fight could be had on the ice. Those were the rules, hard and fast.

I was old enough to sit with the big guys in the warming house. One of them might throw a handful of snow onto the stove top to watch it sizzle. That was usually the only time Mr. Swanson looked up from his magazine. The warming-house smells — the combined stench of wool mittens and leather choppers, both overheated while hanging on the iron railing that ringed the stove — moist, musty and foul. They were "choppers," not gloves. Only Jack Fredericksen (RHS '55) wore gloves when he skated. That was the second thing that made him different from the rest of us. He wore figures skates, but we couldn't tease him because he was tough. (A few years later, we would wear gloves on winter dates when we got the family car.)

We often stayed too long inside the warming house, next to the stove. We were either teasing a girl or flirting with her — often the former being part of the latter — and we sweated our way back out onto the ice.

Hockey skates were more popular than speeds at Keewaydin and Longfellow. Sibley kids wore both kinds. The choice at Hiawatha was speed skates — my CCMs. That meant we had to look cool and not lose our balance as we clump-clumped our long blades across the wooden flooring of the warming house to the exit door and the ramp down onto the ice.

1951 City Hockey (Cub Division) champs.
*Minnehaha Falls Athletic Club. **Front row:** Don Swanson,*
Doug Hansen, (unknown), Doug Larson, Jim Keeley, (unknown).
***Back row:** Ron Johnson, John Hrkal, Jerry Shetler (RHS '55),*
Richard Tollefsbol. Courtesy Doug Larson.

The girls fared better, looking like ballerinas as they tilted toward the door on the toe-toothed blades of their spotless-white figure skates.

I actually tried figure skates a couple of times, but did not like the "catchy toes," which tended to put a novice on his nose, more than once.

CHARLES GUDMUNSON

I started with figure skates and loved them. I could even do a swan, was pretty good, figure eights, etc. Then the "Silver Skates" competition came to Hiawatha. Joanne Johnson won the first year. I won the second year. Butch [Born] loaned me his speed skates for the big race at Powderhorn. I came in second and won my own speed skates. My parents would put the porch light on [across the street] when I needed to go home. I could pretend I didn't see it, but many on the rink and in the warming house would tell me.

CAROL PETERSON

[At Sibley] both a flooded field and a hockey rink gave all of us the opportunity to become ice skaters. My two brothers were adequate, but, frankly, I was lousy. My mother attributed it to "weak ankles" (whatever that meant), but I knew I just sucked. Some of the kids were terrific, like Bob Carlson [RHS '57], who just whizzed by us. I was so poor a skater that I couldn't think of participating in anything but holding onto the nearest support. Our biggest fear was falling on the ice, having a head injury and dying, something we had heard about somewhere else in the city. I still keep a pair of adult ice skates here in southern Arizona, but my wife, Gerry, periodically seeks to dispose of them. I have no intention of doing so, since it remains part of my (meager) heritage.

RONALD PETERSON

Sibley ice-skating! I spent a lot of evenings and afternoons at Sibley, skating for fun. I enjoyed it a lot; the speed and the maneuverability especially. We played a lot of games. Most of them involved outskating or outspeeding the opponents. Some involved heckling the girls. But some of them were pretty quick, so they played prisoner's base and/or pom-pom-pullaway with the boys. Just about all the boys had hockey skates, and the girls wore figure skates. I remember a couple of girls who had speed skates, but they generally went to Powderhorn Park where the racers hung out. Same with the boys. I got some "speeders" and tried them for a while, but didn't really care for them. I remember trying to outrun a girl at the Minnehaha Falls rink, she on speed skates and me with my old hockeys. She kicked my butt like I was out there on street shoes. If I had thoughts of romance, they were immediately nullified by my inability to perform well.

CHARLES GUDMUNSON

Sibley Park had a separate hockey rink on the east side of the park with boards. The main skating area was the baseball fields flooded with water from the park building. They also would put up a temporary warming house with a wood-burning stove, benches for changing skates, storage for your boots, and wooden stairs to walk on down to the skating area. We had a combination of skates — speed skates and hockey — more hockey in elementary school and then speed skates in junior-high years. Definitely not figure skates! Pretty much the same tag games that kids at other rinks played. A few bullies would either bump into you so you would lose your balance and fall down, or throw snow balls at you. We could always go tell the attendant and he would skate after them and give one last warning or they were done skating.

JOSEPH STEINER

Fond memories of the skating days at Hiawatha. Pom-pom-pullaway and crack the whip. My most cherished memory is skating with Chubby Grady to the "Tennessee Waltz" by Patti Page. It was a real joy to have a boy ask you to skate with him. I remember the smells in the warming house. The girls did the figure eights on the ice. Arlo [Arloine Dolan] broke her wrist one winter. I don't remember how it happened. We walked to her house from the ice rink. It was such an innocent time. We could walk to and from the rink and not worry, although, I think my mom probably did do it a bit, especially if we had to walk alone. New skates for Christmas was a big deal.

JANE HAGEN

It seemed like there were a lot of minor injuries … a lot of them hurt feelings. Some for falls, of course. Then there were collisions between the "thugs" playing prisoner's base and little kids just barely moving. Nothing serious, but sometimes the mothers came after us with vengeance in mind. As I remember it, we listened to the wailing of the mom for what we considered an appropriate amount of time, apologized profusely, offered to hold up the kid and take him around the rink. Then, when all appeared calm for both mother and child, we disappeared into the warming house. Good times! Good memories!

CHARLES GUDMUNSON

Some didn't have the benefit of living near public ice-skating rinks.

We had a vacant lot next to ours, and my dad would flood much of it when the temperature went down so we and many neighborhood kids could skate. Later, when a house was built next door, we had to walk to the ice rink on the lagoon side of Nokomis.

JORUN OLSON

When the older kids tired of nighttime skating, they went car hopping. Guptil's corner, over on 42nd, was one of the best spots for doing it.

The hoppers delighted in a trick they had developed. They'd hide behind the grocery store and wait for a car to pull up at the stop sign. No one jumped out from the crowd to grab onto a bumper. Instead, as the car began to move away, they all yelled out, "Hang on, Billy, hang on!" The driver would slam on his breaks, skidding a bit, jump out and run around to the rear of his car to grab the little brat. No car hopper, no brat.

But when you did the real hop, timing was important. You wanted to grab the bumper as soon as the car started to move away from its stop. Most cars didn't really stop. They slowly slid their way through the intersection once they saw no headlights coming from the cross street. But if the car didn't move right away, you didn't. Your boots might settle in to a "hold" — not good — and you'd be sucking exhaust right up into your face. You wanted a clean "grab and go."

> Hopping cars — latching onto slow-moving vehicles in the snow and sliding along for a ways was just part of growing up. It was a winter rite of passage, if you will. You'd wait for a car at a stop sign and jump on when they started up. In the days when cars had bumpers (both front and rear and long-since gone), holding onto the rear, which put you below the back-window view, was just plain fun. There was always a danger playing with a

moving vehicle but I never heard of anyone injured by the practice. You would do it at night, with good snow on the ground and in a residential neighborhood far from busy streets. Even if the car sped up you could let go safely on the snow-covered streets. Our favorite place was around Sibley Field, an area where several stop signs could be found. While I still think of it as harmless, I'm glad my kids never had the opportunity to do it.

RONALD PETERSON

A couple of older kids showed me how car hopping was done: Begin with hard-packed snow on a side street, preferably with a stop sign at one intersection. Car stops for the sign; hopper sneaks up behind the car, grabs hold of the bumper, hangs on and goes zipping down the street, letting go when the next stop sign is coming up or the driver signals for a turn. Very cool, eh? Engineer's boots slid well across the packed snow and also kept the snow from going up the pants leg. One night, however, I had made a good "capture," and the car and I tore down 25th Avenue at about 35 mph. A real thrill. I had not done a good recon job, though, so I was not aware of the bare manhole cover in the middle of the street (snow had melted off it). I hit exposed steel and asphalt. The boots were of no use after that. They simply joined my body in flopping around like a beached sunfish as I continued down the street at 35 mph. Yikes! Did that ever hurt.

CHARLES GUDMUNSON

Some "captures" went the other way.

> …the time that one driver stopped, got out of his car and chased us down. Unfortunately, I slipped and fell during the chase. He caught me and slapped me around a few times. Since he was bigger than me, there was not much I could do but take it. The incident did slow our hopping for a few days, but soon we were back in action. This activity started in February, as soon as the skating rinks closed, and lasted until the streets were clean, usually in late March.
>
> DOUGLAS LARSON

Imagine the look on the driver's face the next morning when he sees a pair of choppers frozen to his rear bumpers.

> With choppers, if the wettish leather froze on the bumper you could slip your hands and linings out and be free.
>
> JOSEPH STEINER

Junior-high girls didn't hop cars, not even the bravest of the tomboys. They stayed home nights and baked cookies to win Girl Scout merit badges. They wrote love notes to pass in the hallway the next day, and whispered to each other on the phone. Maybe ironed for the next day.

Minnehaha Falls with ice and snow.
Photo courtesy of Minnesota Historical Society.

PART III

December 1950 broke cold and stayed that way. A record snowfall, the radio said. I was eleven and a half years old. The "half" was important. On one of the Christmas vacation days, John Pollard, my best friend over on 43rd, and I went down into the Deer Pen in Minnehaha Park.

We started out by sledding down the baby hills by the creek. Once we'd built up enough courage, we joined other kids who were going down the steeper hills closer to the ski jump. We left our Flexible Flyers at the bottom and walked up footholds in the narrow wooden planking set into the hillside. We usually came back down on big sheets of cardboard. For some kids those were the only "sleds" they had.

Sometimes, we went over to the toboggan run, bundled ourselves together on one of them and came down. Usually one kid brought a toboggan down to the Pen. Maybe his dad had money. I looked down the hill. I was a little scared. My mom had taught me how to pray, but I didn't think it was meant for toboggan rides.

I said a quick one anyways and jumped on. We barreled down the hill, holding onto each other or the rope lines strung along the sides of the toboggan, ending up in a train wreck of brown parkas at the bottom. Any fright we may have felt we held in — not like the girls. They screamed all the way down. Like girls. But we never saw many of them down there in the Pen — at least not in the winter.

The ski jump. On this particular day, a few jumpers were going off of it. We stared up. They collected in the little staging box at the top. One jumper down at the bottom threw his skis over his shoulder and walked over to the planking to go back up the hill. He spoke English kinda funny.

I looked at him. And, in a fantasy moment — I'm going up there to be with them all.

With Bjorn and Engvold, big guys with ski jumper names. You bet! I wave to my friends down below who are looking up at me. They wave back. I check my bindings and wait my turn to go down the chute. I'm a little tense. I grip the worn railing and then execute a release. Dropping fast in a tuck I'm going down the snow-packed slide, picking up speed. From a crouch, I spring open at the edge of the ramp and lift off into the late afternoon sky, my ski tips straight up, in perfect parallel. My body pushes forward, leaning against the wind — a photo moment any Finn would envy. I come down in a textbook one-knee telemark landing, and hear the cheers of onlookers lined up four-deep on both sides. In Norwegian or Swedish, they shout the equivalent of "Yah, he nailed that one, he did!"

Just a fantasy. But some kids, a few years older and many years braver than I, tried it when there was no jump competition going on. Most of those who dared the jump bumped and skidded their way down the hill, ass over teakettle — skis freed from the skier, one flying off to the left, the other scooting down the hill. The ski-less skier, once he bottomed out at the base of the hill, jumped up, raised his arms and did a victory dance. Jimmy

Dykstra, braver than his years should've allowed, made the jump with no real jump bindings, just leather straps.

Our football coach, Mr. Armstrong, went off once, on barrel staves, dressed as a clown. At the ski meets, sometimes his was the only name I could pronounce — unlike Hakonnen and Skovde. They came over from the big ski jumps at Bush Lake and Wirth to compete in Deer Pen events.

> I was skiing and sledding in the Deer Pen through most of my days at Hiawatha School. I was in seventh grade at Sanford Junior High when my buddy and fellow classmate Tom Tanner decided to start ski jumping in the Pen. We took our old, worn-out skis and went jumping. We were fearless but finally graduated to the large, heavy, multi-groove jumping skis. We also jumped at Bush Lake and Wirth Park. One warm day at the Pen, the snow was melting fast on the landing hill. The Park Board was scraping snow off the lakes and dumping it on the landing hill so we could have a tournament. I was the first to jump and landed on the new snow. I stuck on the wet snow and went over the front of my skis and landed on my head. I don't remember the walk home but do remember the time spent in the hospital with a concussion. The jumping lasted through ninth grade and was never attempted again.

JAMES C. MEYERS

We sledded down hills with a lot of kids from other neighborhoods. We didn't know them, but they also went to schools with Indian names, like Minnehaha or Keewaydin. We Hiawatha kids were tough. We weren't ascared of kids from other neighborhoods. Me and my pal were both eleven and a half years old that winter, twelve if anyone asked. If things got close to a fight, we'd say we had older brothers at home, so they'd better be careful "My big brother can beat up your big brother."

But if a fight did happen in those days, it did so under certain ground rules. One only fought someone who was in the same grade in school. Or maybe one grade off. Those were the rules, hard and fast. Word got around if you won a fight against someone who was one or two grades ahead of you. Especially if someone double-dared you to do it.

I never met anyone in the Deer Pen from St. Paul. They never came across the bridge. I don't think I knew any kids from over there until I was in high school and met a few from Cretin and St. Thomas Academy. I guess the City Fathers on each side never really got along — the Swedes and Germans on our side of the river and the Irish over there. On our share of the Ford Bridge, the road was paved out mid-span, where it gave way to an all-brick surface coming from the St. Paul side.

When the park lights came on at the bottom of the Pen, it was time to go home. No moms waited in cars to meet us after we got to the top of the stone steps. Ours probably didn't even know where we were. In those days, we never had to ask for permission to go anywhere. We were just out of the house, out playing, out.

Then the one-mile trudge back home. We dragged our sleds across the parkway and over the snow-piled field to where 44th dead-ended into Nawadaha Boulevard. The snow started up again so I couldn't make out the boarded-up pony ride concession over to the left at the edge of the park. There, a few summers earlier, I had busted a high-spirited bronco, one that probably had been in a few cowboy and Indian serials up at the Falls Theater. I think my older brother held the reins — at my dad's insistence — and walked me and my steed around the circle.

Longfellow Library was farther west across Hiawatha Avenue, which I couldn't see even on a clear day from where we stood.

We crossed 46th, the widest street I had known up to then. I looked a few blocks over to my right and saw the shuttered Rich 'O Root Beer stand on the corner. They'd put a "closed for winter" sign in the counter window in early November. From that corner, the road turned and became Ford Parkway up to the bridge and over to the assembly plant in St. Paul.

At the other end of the street, to the west, I could barely make out the lights at the Northern Lumber yard in the falling snow. My dad bought his lumber at Northern for the woodworking projects he spent a lifetime on in the basement. We never saw him after supper. Maybe to get away from my mom, who did all the talking in the family.

Cold and tired, I had yet to learn how to swear, so I just said it was darn cold. (I knew "darn" wasn't a swear word. My mom heard me say it once and she didn't reach for the wooden ruler with the metal liner she kept in the kitchen drawer.) Funny, how fingers got even colder when hands stopped playing and just ended up pulling a sled. I was in the last of my mittens stage, a few years before I would own a pair of choppers, and well before I would wear leather gloves. Maybe I wore long underwear on that cold day, but I wouldn't tell anyone, not even John that day. He wouldn't tell me if he wore any, either.

We had to keep moving to keep our feet from getting even colder. The few times we stopped to let a car pass, we'd stomp them down in the snow while we stood aside.

I didn't know how cold it was, maybe ten above or ten below. We were too young to care or think about numbers. Or to consult the weather ball, on top of a bank building downtown, that they'd put up the year before. That was for grown-ups. But it was as cold as it was one day at St. Helena's. I was waiting outside for my mom and dad after the children's mass to come out of the parents' mass upstairs. Two older kids came up to me and offered me a quarter if I dared put my tongue on the frozen iron railing that led up to the front doors of the church. I didn't do it, although the quarter would've felt nice in my pocket going home that day.

We just went outside, long before "wind chill" became a phrase. I remember one time — it was close to thirty below — I saw a kid over on the Hiawatha rink trying to move on his Christmas morning skates. His blades went "clank, clank," as if he were skating on a big steel plate. My dad said that if it's too cold out the blades couldn't melt the ice as they passed over, and skates can't skate. I didn't understand that, but I had to believe him. He was my dad.

There were few outdoor smells in the winter. Nothing rotted along the curbs or in the gutters. Everything was locked in, under snow, waiting for spring. Then, things smelled again — moist earth that had come back from the dead, grass, fresh rain, wet dogs, fried onions from an open kitchen window, spilled gasoline in a driveway. Later came the summer and fall smells — broken-up street tar and burning leaves. The nose was "on hold" all winter. Maybe you caught a whiff of exhaust from a passing car, or lingering smoke from someone's cigarette, but that was it. Smells in the air were flat and dull. And the air that you took in was cold. It stung. We took only shallow breaths — only what was needed — then exhaled white sprays of it back out through our mouths.

Chimney smoke didn't smell, unless it was from the burning logs of someone's fireplace. But we never got that smell along 44th. That came from the fancy houses farther down toward the river, where the streets curved. I never knew why they just couldn't keep warm, as we did, from baseboard vents that brought the heat up from a coal-burning furnace.

But your nose caught smells when it came in from the cold, like inside Mr. Swanson's warming house at the skating rink at Hiawatha. Nothing back outside, unless you picked up a whiff of a Clove or Blackjack stick that somebody had just put in their mouth.

Colors. We didn't have many in the winter. Blacks and browns and dirty snow — soot-dusted by furnace smoke. And the skies got dark early. Bright days went away for weeks, or at least the blue parts and the puffy clouds. So many things went away in the winter — colors, smells, dogs, cats and flowers — I wished we could go away. We had to stay behind. The sparrows in our backyard stayed too. They were either very brave or too dumb to fly south like the robins.

At the end of each block, overhead lamps cast down a warm amber glow onto the intersections. Yellow snow. Everything else around us was cold white, but for the shiny red stripes on the sleds, and the occasional yellow streetcar two blocks over. Cars' colors were a few years away.

We stayed out in the street, heads down, tracing the tire-chain marks of the last passing car, few as they were. A few winters later, I would follow those same tire tracks in the predawn darkness on my big-basket-in-front Schwinn bike, delivering the *Tribune*. John had a Monarch.

We were on the same street we would come back down in the early spring thaw. Again, with our heads down, but then we'd be searching along the curbs and in gutters for nickels and dimes, or even quarters, that people getting out of cars over the winter had dropped into the deep snow. Of course, the big money was found on the Hiawatha grounds and rink after the huge late-March melt.

But spring was a long way off. We hunkered down, our heads deep into the hoods of bulky brown parkas with fake-fleece lining, staring numbly as we walked. Minnesota had geese, but down feathers never found their way into those jackets. I swear, that winter I saw a Fox Movietone newsreel at the Riverview that showed that same parka being worn by a North Korean POW.

My mom probably got mine at the Sears over on Lake Street and Chicago, or much closer to our house, at Freeman's. Later, grown-ups wore similar coats without hoods. They called them car coats. We wore overshoes with the thin curved-slotted buckles that were supposed to snap shut but kept breaking off. Some of the older guys in the neighborhood had zippered ones. One guy always wore his unzipped so the sides flared out as he walked down the street. That was cool.

But for an occasional car, the streets were empty. So cold-quiet-cold, only the monotonous clink-clinking of snow chains on the tires of the few approaching cars — street chimes. We heard them coming, no need to honk. We stepped aside again to let them pass. White exhaust fanned up into our faces, warming us for a few seconds as we coughed through it. Then we continued at a pace that had become mechanical — three steps, three pulls on the sled, two more feet down the street.

Another car passed. Two older kids were hanging onto the back bumper and giggling their way down the street. Hoppers. I stared at them. I would have to learn how to hop cars. In a few years, I'd be out there doing it.

As with smells and colors, there were few sounds in the winter. The neighborhood was under a muffled lock-down. December had no outdoor noise — not like Aquatennial Sundays, when you could hear the sounds all the way over from boats racing on Lake Nokomis. Just a stillness, even as we walked, but for the "thwick, thwick" of our frozen corduroys. Or the sounds that came from the snow shovels scraping the sidewalks. Just a few of those sounds, though. Most shovelers left a hardened layer of snow, just above the bare pavement. That was it. The snow blankets were everywhere. Quiet. We were squeezed in between giant ear muffs.

I looked over when I heard a streetcar down on 46th. Streetlights made the icicles hanging below the motorman's window look like crystal necklaces.

We saw Christmas tree lights in some windows. It was a neighborhood of Christians (or pretenders, some of them, I guess) with manger scenes under their trees.

I remember one house had a gold star on a card hanging against the window. It had hung there up till last year. Maybe she had refused to take it down after the war. To remind her neighbors. Now it was gone. Maybe she was, too.

There were a few houses with no lights on at all, come suppertime, and we thought that was strange. Where were the people, the grown-ups? It was too cold for them, or for girls, to be outside. Or for that matter, even dogs. But I remembered my mom telling me that some people drained their pipes, closed their homes and went to Florida when it got really cold. No one in our neighborhood had money to do that, unless they lived on Edmund Boulevard and drove their kids to private schools. I wondered why they had to do that. I thought Hiawatha was a good school with a big playground next to it.

Through the falling snow we could see the lights still on at

Tidlunds' (Dave, RHS '55, Don, RHS '56) two blocks over. It was one of the few grocery stores in our little corner pocket of south Minneapolis — blocked by the river and the Falls. It was across the street from a small out-of-place farm. Sheltering Arms was down the field toward the river. It was too bad that the kids lying in those beds that day didn't have the kind of fun we'd just had down in the Deer Pen.

We kept going. A block up, we stopped and watched three guys shouting at the driver of a snow-stuck car. They were trying to push it out of a snowbank. We listened. Each one had different advice.

The snowdrifts, either from the blowing wind or the plows, never got that high in later years. Maybe that was due to fewer heavy snowfalls or because I would never be four-foot-eleven again. There were times when I wondered if I would ever get taller than those snowbanks, even though I saw progress when my mom penciled in my growth on the kitchen door frame. But when we finally grew taller we made good use of piled-up snow, particularly those along 42nd on the way home from junior high school. We thirteen-year-olds pushed the girls into them — Jane, Carol Pete, and Arloine. We called it flirting.

As we went down the street toward home, we couldn't see if someone had ducked down on the sidewalk behind a snow-banked boulevard[7] waiting to throw a snowball. Not to worry. The snow was too cold to pack a good one. It had to melt a little

[7]For some odd reason we in Minneapolis called the narrow tree-lined strip of grass that ran down the block between the curb and sidewalk a "boulevard."

so it would hold itself together in flight. Snow, that day, was just fluff in a thrower's hands.

Odd, how it always took longer to get home than it did to go down there in the morning. It was as if we'd taken a different route. We passed through another intersection and came up to Hiawatha playground. We knew we were close to home. The water fountain was gone. The Park Board dismantled it every November.

By now I could see the smoke curling up white from our chimney in the next block. It was a welcoming sight. My dad was worried that the coal man might not make it through the snow if we ran out. A few minutes later I looked up again, and the smoke was in the same spot over the house — frozen in the air — too cold to curl away. My house was a still-life painting, a Christmas card.

I saw the Christmas-tree lights through our dining-room window. All blue ones. My mom had collected enough of them from other strings. She said that the non-blue bulbs had burned out or were broken. So she said.

My dad teased her, saying that she threw a lot of them into the trash when we weren't looking. By that December she had met her goal — a tree with only blue lights. She said it gave out a nice winter look. As if we needed that.

We passed the Bergquist place down the block. The grown-ups in that house were always yelling at each other, so loud that we could hear them up and down the block in the summer.

When their windows were open, we sneaked up and listened and giggled underneath the screens until a neighbor shooed us away. Now, we couldn't hear anything, although we guessed they still lived there, shouting behind closed windows.

Then, it was on to Merlin White's house, the Augsburg quarterback. It was too cold for him to be out washing his car, which he did every Saturday morning in the summer. Behind his garage, a year or so later, Dickie would show me how to inhale a cigarette.

The snowflakes were bigger now. That meant the snowfall would soon end.

Almost home, we moved on, glancing over at the few kids daring the cold and skating under the outdoor lights of the rink. The snow from the record fall had been plowed so high onto the banks that we could only see the heads of the skaters. Maybe they were playing pom-pom-pullaway or prisoner's base, though we were still too young to know how those games were played. A few years later, that's where we would spend the late afternoons and evenings of our winters, learning those games and discovering speed skates and girls — in that order. (My dad would hang the sled that I was pulling that night on a hook in a wall in the garage. To remain there. For good.)

Girls. As for them, well, I knew they were a little like us but — then again — not exactly. I didn't have any sisters, so I couldn't tell. But they were just different. Their "insides" were. (I had overheard a kid use that word when he talked about girls down in the woods.) It was a good way to say it. But I didn't know just *how* their insides were different. I knew I'd find that out when the time came. That winter I was still at an age where I didn't have to understand girls, or have much to do with them.

To get to know about them I would have to start somewhere. And that somewhere was in front of the magazine shelves at Holm drugstore. The insides? Hah! I didn't even know much about their outsides. The magazines weren't much help. The girls were pretty much covered up. So, too, some of the magazines. Brown paper wrappings.

> Lockner's Drugs at 38th Street and Bloomington Avenue was the hub of daily life. Back in the corner were the girlie magazines. Although not "old enough" to go back and browse, we would stand around the rack long enough to see the fleshy parts of pretty women.
>
> PAUL WULKAN

But there were some things I knew for certain. They couldn't do a lot of things right, like run or throw a snowball. They even wore the buttons on the wrong side of their coats. And in the summer they couldn't hit a softball or play knife games over on the playground. All they did was skip rope. We guys had more fun.

But one thing I was sure about girls — teachers always favored them.

We came up along the tennis courts across from my house. The tall fence was layered almost halfway up with new snow. Funny how I thought that snow in November and December blew into the city. By January it got tired of blowing and just fell. And fall it did, the new white stuff settling on piles of old snow, covered with chocolate ice-cream sprinkles from the coal smoke.

We pulled our sleds over onto my corner sidewalk and jumped them over the little strip of unshoveled snow that my older brother left for me. He always claimed that it belonged to my part of the household division of labor. Of course, I knew it belonged to him. Mom was the snow-shoveling supervisor. She would stand at the dining-room window and point to the spot on the snow-covered sidewalk where one son's shovel duties ended and the other son's began. The windows were always sealed with frost. I don't think she could see through them very well.

John went over to his house, and I threw myself against the back door of mine. I snow-stomped my way into the rear hallway, next to the refrigerator that I still called an icebox. Finally, I could defrost and unbuckle my overshoes.

Thinking back, I never went in or out of my house through the front door, even in the summer. The only time I went into the enclosed front porch off the living room was to check the floor below the mail slot for the little brown packages from the cereal people. My name was the only one printed on the labels — not "in care of" some parent — but to me. If I ate enough of their cereal I could order things like a glow-in-the-dark spy decoder ring with a secret compartment or a model rocket ship. I scotch-taped quarters to two boxtops and sent off the envelope to Battle Creek, Michigan, with absolute and unconditional reliance on the promises printed on the backs of their boxes.

When a package arrived, I wouldn't announce it to any members of my family. I just took the little box to my room and opened it in the privacy of the moment. My parents, even my brother, wouldn't understand the excitement I felt that someone "out east" had remembered me in his very busy life.

Home. It meant a lot of things to me, some of which I would not realize and appreciate until years later. One of the things it did mean to me on that December night was that I had arrived just in time to listen to my favorite program on the small Admiral in the kitchen while we ate supper. Just in time to hear Brace Beemer, in that voice that sounded like someone shouting up from the basement when a door had been left open — "A fiery horse with the speed of light, a cloud of dust and a hearty 'Hi-Yo, Silver,' *The Lone Ranger!*"

PART IV

*Just one more time. I want to hear that night sound — beyond
the mating-call chirping of the crickets in the backyard — of
a night-shift streetcar, moving on the tracks. Listen to it through the
bedroom screen... slow down... pause... then glide-start back
up again, wheels on tracks, grinding steel-on-steel, soon to turn
north at 42nd and recede into the distance on its way down to 38th,
an echo from our early years — the last summer night sound
just before I fall asleep. Just one more time.*

1

One summer Saturday morning, Bobby and I walked down
to our streetcar stop at the end of our block. We were going
downtown, away from our neighborhood — an adventure. It was
something we could talk about later that night.

We had to avoid the cracks on the small concrete sidewalk
squares — "step on a crack and break your mother's back." They
were old, some tipped up by the push of tree roots underneath.
Tough on the knees of fallen roller skaters.

A lot of them were stamped with the name of the paving
contractor before the concrete hardened. Each summer, batches
of them were pulled up and repaved with larger squares until the
block-long sidewalk was updated. Our block was being modern-

ized. Bobby pointed out his initials, which he'd carved the summer before when a new pour was made.

We also had to step around dog poop. One was white. I thought it came from the neighbor's dog two houses over from us — white-haired. A dog came out from the side of a house without an owner. No need. It walked itself and knew how to get home to its bowl. It stopped, looked at me and Bobby, and crossed the street. Turned onto another front yard and disappeared.

The old man who had moved in across the street a few months ago was doing his morning walk down the sidewalk. He was just looking around at the houses, hands clasped behind his back. He was Swedish. My dad always greeted him with, "Good morning, Governor." Dad would say that when he didn't know a man's name — out of respect, he'd say. (I think it was a British thing.) I heard they were called, "ocean crossers."[8] There was another one farther down on the block. When we went house-to-house selling Christmas cards, that one grunted and nodded as he fumbled around with English when he answered the doorbell.

We passed by Bobby's place, where we used to sit on his front steps and see who could hold his breath the longest.

A man was standing at the back of his ice truck, chopping a block with an ice pick. He was big. A red face dripped with sweat.

---

[8]My dad was an ocean crosser. Orphaned in Scotland (Glasgow-born, Irish heritage) at age thirteen, he crossed a few years later in 1919 to join a sister on a farm in Amery, Wisconsin. A few years after that, he moved to Minneapolis. He laughed when he told the story of coming out from his naturalization ceremony at the downtown courthouse. A Swedish woman from a group of volunteers came up to him and gave him a tiny American flag and a printed schedule of biweekly "How to Speak English" classes.

He hooked into a huge chunk, turned and swung it onto a rubber pad draped over his shoulder and lugged it up to and around the side of the Grandlund's house to a back door.

Mahre Bros Service (included ice sales), 38th and Cedar.
Courtesy Joanne (Mahre) Haugen.

My dad was the "ice man" in our neighborhood. That made our back alley a gathering place on hot summer afternoons when he and his truck would arrive home. We scampered up on the wooden floor covered in slivers and leftover chunks of ice to chew on them and cool off.

JOANNE MAHRE

One of my earliest memories is the ice man coming every few days when I was a preschooler. This was before the days of a refrigerator. My mother would put a cardboard sign in a front window, telling the ice man how much ice to bring to our house. As I remember, it was most often the bigger number "50" (pounds) that showed to the street. He wore a black rubber cape. He picked the block of ice up with a pair of giant tongs, hefted it over his shoulder, and brought it to the back door and then into the ice box. In the hot summer, we would enjoy picking up the ice chips that fell in his wake.

RUTH JOHNSON

I looked up and down 44th. The street was straight — not a curve in sight. Houses on those streets would have views of Lake Harriet or Calhoun or even Minnehaha Creek from their front window. And if you lived there, your dad probably had money.

We walked past an unbroken line of one-story bungalows with low-pitched roofs, fourteen on my side of the block, except for a "pushed-back" house set on the lot against the alley. An old couple lived there. I always wondered who cut their grass. The houses all looked the same, stucco-white with green or brown trimming.

Pretty much the same on the inside — a little vestibule before you walked into a living room with an easy chair and sofa, into a dining room where the people didn't dine, a kitchen beyond that, then two bedrooms off to the right with a bathroom in between. The door off our kitchen opened to a patchy-grass and pounded-dirt backyard. Any "finished" attics were done so at the hands of the owners.

The builders intended that the houses be one story of living space, the unheated attic with exposed rafters meant for attic stuff. Yes, I thought attics were for those things and not for two healthy growing boys. They should be "healthy and growing" elsewhere, down on the floor of the house intended by the builder for the living, to be in rooms warmed by furnaces in the winters and ventilating fans in the summers. But that was not in my dad's plans.

One day, he looked around the living room and came across two boys who had outgrown their bedroom on the first floor. Other dads with young boys (and some with girls) had the same thoughts, and their offspring were sent "upstairs" to live in varying degrees of comfort or discomfort. One day my brother and I were moved to our "refurbished" attic. It had two beds, a dresser, and a small rug, alongside attic things — trunks of moth-balled clothes, cardboard boxes filled with Christmas decorations and light bulbs, albums filled with photos of long-since-dead relatives, all set against seldom-used suitcases and never-again-to-be-used baby things.

I can't recall if the moving day occurred in the winter. If so, a sympathetic mom sent up a small space heater to supplement the blankets. If in the summer, we got one of those small revolving G.E. table fans (the kind that Sergeant Ernest Borgnine might've had on his desk in *From Here to Eternity*).

That winter my self pity ran rampant. I imagined throwing "HELP" notes out an attic window, which might flutter down onto the snow close enough to the sidewalk so passersby might see them and warn the child protective agencies in the city. That was before our dad cut a hole in the first-floor ceiling and installed a small vent to let warm air seep up from the floor where the grown-ups lived. I decided not to write the note.

By the first spring, we had dropped our demands that more blankets be sent up to our "penal colony." What we really wanted was to be allowed to listen to radio shows on school nights as late as we did on weekends when we were captivated by *Boston Blackie* and *Gangbusters.*

Then summer came. A beam of sunlight came through the attic window one afternoon, and I saw thousands of little dust devils in mid-flight. Flashlight beams caught them at night. It was a whole galaxy of mites seeking out my mouth and nose. I was convinced that they coexisted with me and my brother up there in our attic outpost — of course, never daring to venture downstairs, where our parents lived.

> When I was born, my dad finished the attic for Al, my brother. Finished is a stretch; he didn't know anything about sheet rocking, and he used the old linotype paper mats used to make the lead printing mats for the presses at the *Star and Tribune.* When Al got married, Dad painted [the attic] for me and made me two headboards. I was happy, as it was my own space. Oh yes, heat. It was a hole in the floor with a register cover. In January, I would lay out my clothes the night before and dash downstairs in the morning to get dressed.
>
> CAROL PETERSON

We had four kids in a two-bedroom house, so yes, my sister and I moved on up to the attic when the second little brother came along. My dad's carpentry skills weren't great, but he made an effort. We had one heat register, but it was still pretty chilly in the winter. I seem to remember wearing long underwear almost constantly during the cold months. And it quite often was miserably hot in the summer. A small rotating fan just couldn't lower the temperature much. The thing my sister and I hated the most, though, was the light switch at the bottom of the stairs (crafted by my dad). One flick of the switch cut off all electricity in the attic: lights, radio, record player, and even the fan. (We lost all control over our lives!) We learned to keep the music low (battery-powered radio), and I always kept a flashlight for reading in bed, just in case.

JORUN OLSON

We had three bedrooms upstairs and one down for a five-person family, so I had no garret-like experiences to relate. I do remember popping out of bed during a Minnesota winter and hitting my bare feet on an icy-cold floor. The best part of that was my mother placing clean underwear on the radiators, an unbelievably bliss-ful event.

RONALD PETERSON

A portion of our attic had been refurbished into a comfortable bedroom and, because I was five years older than my brother, I got the upstairs bedroom. The room was decorated nicely, but it was much colder than the rest of the house in the winter and much warmer in the summer. I got in the habit of sleeping under five blankets during the winter, and it took me quite a while to get over associating weight with warmth. In the summer, my room would often become so insufferably hot that I would sleep on a daybed in the sun porch off the living room. This was fine except in the morning, when, if they'd wanted to, the whole neighborhood could have seen me getting out of bed.

CYNTHIA KERSTEN

Our dad was a post office worker, but most Saturdays and evenings he turned carpenter. Did work for friends to fix up *their* attics, basements and whatever needed help. Oh, yes, our house had attic space, too. No bathroom but all across the back of our house he built two bedrooms with dormers. My two brothers were in one, and I in the other. The upstairs hallway was finished with bookshelves and cabinets, and across from my brothers' room was a door into the front half of the attic, freezing cold in winter and hotter than blazes in summer. Our bedrooms were well insulated and comfortable. Also, floor grates brought heat into our bedrooms from below. Our little princess (sister), eight years younger than I (ten and twelve years younger than our brothers) took over that other first-floor bedroom. She moved to mine in later years.

Arloine Hullar

The front doors of the houses on our block were seldom used — buttoned up they were. Ours was reserved for Halloween kids, Christmas relatives, Jehovah's Witnesses and, "Mom! It's the Watkins man." (I think we got some kind of chest rub for colds in a round green tin.) Yes, and for Clem Bauer (RHS '52) the paper boy on his collection rounds.

We were a back-door family. All our socializing life went on in the back — backyards, back doors, garages and back alleys — back everything. Some families had backyard chicken and pigeon coops. The moms and dads talked over backyard fences with their neighbors. Whoever heard of a front-yard fence? They talked, that is, if the two families were on speaking terms. If not, they let the bushes on the property line grow high.

> The back doors were always open to kids in our neighborhood.
>
> Ruth Johnson

The back doors were off the kitchens, where most of the moms spent their time — when they were not washing, cleaning, ironing, sewing, mopping, polishing, and sometimes scolding. We really only got to know the mothers. Not until years later, at night football games at Sibley, did we finally see the dads.

We didn't really know the people behind the doors if no kids lived in the houses. (Anyone in his or her mid to late teens was no longer a "kid" and didn't count.) But we'd heard about some of the people in those houses.

> When I was filling orders for my Camp Fire donuts house to house, I took one from an old codger (probably the age I am now) on 46th Avenue, who had a reputation of being a drunk. My dad had loaded the donuts into his car (I'd sold 100 dozen), and I warned him that this customer might give me trouble. The guy did in fact urge me to come into his house in spite of my protests. My dad had to come to the door to extricate me, and I realized I had been exposed to a seamier side of life than I was used to.
>
> CYNTHIA KERSTEN

> Mr. Johnson, who lived two houses down, would go for walks in August with his long black winter coat, hat and gloves on. Then there was my next-door neighbor. One day he went to his garage, shut the door and started his car, sat in it and never woke up.
>
> JOSEPH STEINER

Often, the closest anyone got to see inside the pulled-shades and drawn-curtain houses were the paperboys, a few of them wary of going up to doors on their collection rounds. And it seemed like every neighborhood had a "cat lady."

Some four houses up the street on a small hill lived the Greek Cat Lady. She had all her shades pulled down all the time. The only time anyone got a glimpse of her was when she let her cats out. She was always dressed in black, with a black shawl over her head — her hands and face, a pale white. Nobody knew anything about her. Then I got the neighborhood paper route with her house included. So I would be the first kid to have any contact with her. Yes, I was somewhat scared. Anyway, when I went to collect the money for the paper every two weeks, she would just crack the door and give me the money without saying a word. Now I had gotten the closest to her of any of my friends and survived to talk about it. Then one day, when I was collecting money for the paper, she spoke to me! Asking if I could buy some groceries at the corner store because her husband was ill. WOW! Now what? So I did. When I brought them back to her house she asked if I could help bring them in the house for her. Now I was really starting to get scared. However, I brought the groceries inside and set them on a round table next to a potbellied cooking stove. No words were exchanged between us, and I was super glad to get out of her dark, scary house. Of course, all the kids in the block wanted a firsthand story of what I had experienced. I will never

forget about my encounter with the Greek Cat Lady and
will always wonder how she came to be so unique.

JOSEPH STEINER

Front yards were useless. I don't know who invented them.
Europeans didn't have them; their houses came right up to a
property line, then a courtyard of sorts in back where they lived
out their lives. Smart thinking.

The only thing that went on out in front of our house was
grass-growing. My dad had put down a high-quality grass seed.
He kept watch over it, as did passersby. The phrase "to put on a
front" had real meaning. Early on, I played out on the front-yard
grass. No gang of kids to scuff up the yard. Just me and Marilyn
Grobe (RHS '58) who lived next door. She and I would sit on the
back of her family's dog, a doberman called "Pinchie." For some
reason, it always bit me and not her. I would go screaming into
the house, bleeding from the leg, crying to my mom that it was
unfair that Pinchie always bit me and never her. Later, the dog
moved with its family over to the Minnehaha neighborhood off
Hiawatha Avenue. I still have the bite scars on my legs. I don't
think she ever got any.

The only other thing I recall doing out front was lying on
my back with John Pollard, picking out faces in the clouds.

As for grass-cutting, each family had its rules. Some dads
exempted the daughters if a son or two could handle such manly
chores. Then again — sons or no sons — some families put all
their kids to work.

In my family, the girls (my sister and me) were eight to ten years older than my two little brothers. Our house was on a hill — 13 steps up from the public sidewalk to our front walk. We had a heavy, old wooden-handled push mower that was treacherous when trying to cut grass on our front hill. "Do I go up and down or side to side?" This usually involved the mower sliding down the hill with me hanging onto it. Growing up without power mowers and snow blowers was all part of the fitness program. Very few fat kids in those days. The only good news about mowing (or shoveling snow) was getting out of washing or drying dishes that day.

JORUN OLSON

2

Our neighborhood was the kind that people didn't move away from, or into — one that strengthened the foundations of childhood. It gave us a sense of security.

If you play with someone each day, each week, your little world is shattered if he moves away. Generally our friends remained the same, each Saturday morning, each summer on the playground with the Park Board box, first days each September at Hiawatha and Sanford. Unlike our adult years, when people were always moving away — they from us, or we from them. (The late playwright Arthur Miller said, as Americans, we move so often that "dislocation, maybe, is part of our uneasiness. It implants the feeling that nothing is really permanent.")

I lived with my grandparents until I was eight years old. Then my dad came home from the war, remarried (my mother died when I was three), and we left what I had thought would be the same forever — that is, living with Grandma and Grandpa. We moved to Minneapolis. I never saw my friends again that I had played with from kindergarten through second grade. There were some kids in the new neighborhood south of Lake Nokomis, but all a little younger than me. It was a new, postwar development, not a lot of houses to start with but new ones being built every day. I remember playing with a girl named Donna, but that friendship didn't last long because she got TB and left for the sanitarium in Glen Lake. I don't remember ever seeing her again. I made new friends at Wenonah in third and fourth grade, but two years later, Wenonah was really crowded so all the kids in my neighborhood were bussed to Field Elementary. I was the only fifth grader to go. Two years later, when all my new friends went on to Ramsey Junior High and, later, Washburn High, I left for Nokomis where I had to make new friends all over again. I was the only kid in my grade who came from Field. I did remember Mary Moriarity, Judy Kibby, Mary Ellen LaVelle and Sharon Lieberg, but I was a shy kid and it was hard for me to make new friends. I had probably figured out friendships were temporary and wouldn't last long.

JORUN OLSON

But for some, frequent dislocation just meant new friends.

From the time I was born until sixth grade, we moved five times, but always in the same south Minneapolis neighborhood, which allowed my two older sisters and me to attend St. Helena for eight years uninterrupted. We lived in rental properties until I was in sixth grade. I remember, once, living in a few upstairs rooms in an old private residence where our family of five shared the bathroom with the owners. I don't know where we all slept. I was small so I think I slept in a crib until I was pretty old. Maybe it stunted my growth considering I'm not much over five feet tall! When I was in sixth grade we moved to our own home up the hill from Longfellow Library but we had six renters — a young family of five and Mrs. Coyne, an old lady — all of whom shared ONE bathroom. All ELEVEN of us! I didn't think it was an unusual or even an inconvenient way to live. I always had wonderful school friends and didn't lack in confidence. I think I was born happy.

GERALDINE BINGHAM

The neighborhood was all pretty much working-class blue collar. If you moved farther south and west, the collars started to get white. Maybe some families on our blocks were poor, but we couldn't tell. And if they had kids, we wouldn't care how much their dads made, only whether they could throw out a runner at first.

I was in Mr. Wheeler's homeroom (at Sanford). As was usual at Christmastime, we had a tree in the room. Somehow I wound up taking the decorations off before we left for Christmas vacation. Mr. Wheeler suggested that we could give the tree to one of the boys in the room. The implication, of course, was that his family wouldn't be able to afford one. I was caught by surprise. Although I knew our neighborhood was a mix of blue-collar and middle-class folks; it had never occurred to me that some families might not be able to purchase a Christmas tree.

CYNTHIA KERSTEN

I didn't think we were poor, even though I only had one doll (Pamela). One girl, Susan Finney, was an only child and had many dolls. One doll was the beautiful Sparkle Plenty, the offspring of the ugly Gravel Gertie and B.O. Plenty from the comic strip Dick Tracy. Well, Sparkle had an incredible wardrobe, and occasionally, Susan would let me dress my doll, Pamela, in one of Sparkle's beautiful dresses.

GERALDINE BINGHAM

3

The dads on our blocks were not outwardly expressive. They didn't hug other men, like Greeks and Italians did. A hand-shake was usually the closest they got to another man's body if he wasn't a brother or a son. No Spanish passion here. Stoic might be the word. And they didn't talk a lot — no appetite for conver-sation. Not like I heard about the Jewish people up on the north side or the Irish across the river. They devoured huge servings of talk. Nor like the Italians either, although my only knowledge of them — mostly from TV shows — was that a lot of them lived in New York City. They talked kind of funny while leaning out second-story windows or sitting on front stoops. The front stoops on our blocks were empty and quiet.

But dads were polite. Going down alleys one got to know people, even grown-ups, and they would greet me — by name — before I had a chance to greet them. Pretty cool. Me, just a kid.

When they worked in their backyards and garages, they never wore gloves. They carried jackknives in their pockets, lit their cigarettes with a match, and left in the morning carrying lunch pails or brown bags. They drank Grain Belt or Hamm's on Saturdays and went to church on Sundays.

Some kids came from families that didn't fit the two-par-ent profile on our blocks. I think there was one single mom on ours. But I heard that her husband didn't come home from the war. Other families lost a parent due to natural causes. Many of the surviving spouses, for whatever reasons, did not remarry. In most cases, the kids in those households turned out just fine. But there were moments of grief and poignancy.

> My father died suddenly and unexpectedly when I was ten years old. He was only forty-one. Life was difficult after my father died. The grief — as well as the financial and social changes — was immediate. There were no grief support groups. In fact, people often believed one should not talk about death. My mother worked, often two jobs, which meant my brother, two years older than I, and I were either alone or in our older sister's care. We had few interactions with other families other than our neighbors(who were great). I was always playing in and out of several of the homes of our neighbors. My good friend, Nancy Erickson, a member of our class, and I had lunch together each day. Her mother died when she was five. The loss of a parent created a bond in our friendship which still exists today.
>
> PAT EIDE

Then there were the few homes with single parents from divorce — but very few, due to the stigma, religious prohibition and economics of divorce.

> There were few divorces when we were children (almost non-existent). We now know there were unhappy families,

but financially, it was difficult for families to separate. Also there was the stigma of divorce. Unfortunately there wasn't much help available for troubled families. People didn't talk about their problems, and counseling was less available, but that too carried a stigma.

PAT EIDE

In my neighborhood, there was only one single mom. Her lifestyle was a little different, but I don't think it disrupted the neighborhood.

CYNTHIA KERSTEN

Most kids had two parents, except for Hovey [James Hovanetz, RHS '57] and me. "Where is your father?" I was asked many times.

DOUGLAS LARSON

One or two of the families on our block had TV sets. We got an Admiral in November 1949, and my brother and I sat on our sofa staring at the "test pattern," wondering what the big deal was. A few months later we watched Monday-night fights from St. Nick's Arena in New York City, all the way to our house. Then, even later, Verne Gagne, Red Bastine and Dirty Dick Raines wrestled in our living room.

It was about that time that televisions were becoming popular, and my dad switched from selling ice to selling

TVs. We had the first one in our neighborhood — about a seven-inch black-and-white, of course. One station came on air for about five or six hours a day. We'd pull the window shades to see the grainy screen better.

JOANNE MAHRE

The corner (38th Street and Bloomington Avenue) was filled with all the basic needs of life, like Peterson's Hardware. We would hurry through dinner to get down there at 6 p.m. and watch *The Lone Ranger.* They put a TV in the window and placed a speaker outside. About ten of us neighborhood kids would sit cross-legged on the sidewalk and watch the weekly episode. At the end of each program, we would gather up and go back home wondering if we would ever have a TV of our own.

PAUL WULKAN

While my aunt had an early TV (which was included in the rental, I believe) our first set was probably about 1950. I remember my mother being upset because a neighborhood boy had seen the set before she had, when it was being delivered — go figure. While my mother was a strong and loving fixture, she was also nuts.

RONALD PETERSON

TV. Our family was one of the last in our neighborhood to own a television set. I remember we rented one for a short time, to see if it would be a worthwhile investment or something our family might use. It was a cube, about twenty inches, but the screen was about six inches. We placed it on a table in the living room (or the "front room," as I remember calling it). We had to sit far away from the screen, nearly into the dining area so we wouldn't damage our eyes. And we could only watch it for a very short time. Programming was only for a limited time anyway, unless you wanted to watch the test pattern. Every so often the screen would go blank or "snowy," and the message "faulty network" would appear.

JORUN OLSON

4

Mrs. Bergstrom came down the sidewalk toward us pushing a baby buggy. We just said hello and kept walking. My mom would always stop and look down inside the carriage and say something nice. I thought that some babies had to be ugly, but I guess she didn't think so.

Babies. We didn't really know where they came from. We were well past all that "stork" stuff but had not made much progress beyond that.

> I recall a discussion in the playground of Bancroft, me and another boy and two girls. The discussion was how babies were delivered. The girls insisted that babies came out of the vagina while we boys could not fathom such a large item coming out of such a small opening. They decided babies must be cut out of the woman. We boys reluctantly conceded to the girls because one of them just had a new baby sister and knew the real facts.
>
> PAUL WULKAN

Some just did the math.

> And I knew zero about sex. I'm not sure who told me but I was pretty disgusted by the whole idea and frankly might not have believed it for a long time. It was easier to

believe in Santa Claus. I was adamant that my mom and dad had sex only three times, resulting in the births of my two sisters and me. God forbid anyone would choose to "do that" unless they absolutely had to! Having only sisters and daughters, I was never privy to "boy stuff." My daughter has three sons, and I've learned more about pre- and adolescent boys as an old lady than I ever did as a younger woman. I don't think I heard the word "penis" until I was an adult. Words like vagina, penis, uterus, pregnant, abortion, intercourse, etc., were never uttered.

GERALDINE BINGHAM

I do remember conversations with girlfriends walking home from junior high, thinking, really? Our parents? They actually did that four times? (Four kids in our family.) Yuck!

JORUN OLSON

The parents, a bit skittish about explaining the "birds and bees" to their children, should have considered sending their eight-year-olds off to farms for the summers, rather than to camps.

We knew nothing. My farm cousins at least had some idea of the way it works and its purpose by observing animals copulating and giving birth. Growing up in the Twin Cities was different.

PAUL WULKAN

Doug [Nash] asked me in fifth grade if I knew the "facts of life." I said sure. He ran around telling everyone on the playground that I said, "I know life is beautiful if we live a clean life." (Lutheran upbringing you know). "What are you talking about?" Too late, everyone was laughing at me.

CAROL THORSON

It was all trial and error, rumor and guesswork. Sex education was what took place in the alleys and playgrounds, and in stories from older kids.

PAUL WULKAN

And then there were the book-loving mothers.

Mom educated me about sex — by giving me a book to read. Having mentioned this to many of my Minneapolis girlfriends, this seemed to be a general pattern. I realize belatedly that this resulted in my concluding that sex wasn't something one talked about. It was definitely hush-hush.

CYNTHIA KERSTEN

We guys had a lot of different opinions in the alley about where babies came from but not one we could all agree on.

5

We got to the corner streetcar stop by Selness's upholstery shop. I glanced down to 46th, to the woods — down where the "Victory Gardens" were a few years earlier.

> We had a triangle-shaped Victory Garden in our backyard. We all helped grow vegetables for our family. Patriotic citizens all over the country had these gardens so that more of the commercial production could go to our soldiers overseas. Forty percent of the vegetables consumed in America during the war was raised in victory gardens in backyards, parks, etc.
>
> RUTH JOHNSON

Woods were almost as important as alleys for growing boys. Every kid deserved to have one in his childhood. That's where the frogs and snakes were.

I had two woods. The "little woods" was a vacant lot down on 46th. When the corn was high, we played hide and seek. One day I was shocked to see that my "hiding and seeking" days had come to a sudden end: the field had been reduced to cornstalk stubble. But according to family rules, I had to continue playing there and not in the more distant "big woods" across the street that led down to River Road.

After pleading with my mom — she was always searching for

a "because" when my "why" quickly followed her "no" — she finally relented. I could cross the street and play there, provided I go with my older brother. His friends called me "tagalong." What excitement! I had left the woods and entered a magic forest — swamps, trees to climb, pussy willows to sharpen into spears, and cigarette-smoking experiment grounds for the older kids. The big woods even had its own hobo. Once he scared me enough that I ran home. I didn't go back for a few days.

Other kids didn't have to go very far from the front steps of their houses to find a patch of woods. As city development moved south toward Wold Chamberlain after World War II, more vacant lots popped up in between the new homes. More "little woods" appeared.

> When we first moved in (late summer before third grade), many of the lots were vacant or undeveloped in our neighborhood. This was probably 1948.
>
> JORUN OLSON

For kids three and a half feet tall, the empty lots, filled with weeds and cornstalks, were a hide-and-seek magical world. That is, until returning G.I.s bought up new homes on them. I can imagine the scene when the new homeowners went knocking on nearby doors to introduce themselves, sometimes with a baby in tow. The moms and dads in the homes would welcome them to their new neighborhood, some adding a "thank you for your service." All the while, two obedient kids would be sulking behind a mother's skirt, eyes downcast, refusing to look up at the "bad people" who took their woods away.

Then, some kids had the best of city living. A farm, all within its limits.

> The city ended, really, at 55th Street. Across the street was Nelson's farm (a swamp and woods nearby). It was owned by two brothers, one of whom was Skeeter Nelson's (RHS '54) dad. I became a regular there. He'd let us help with the milking sometimes, and we could always hang around the barn where they kept Midge and Fanny, their two workhorses. We couldn't ride them, but we got to sit on them from time to time. For an eight-year-old like me, that was a big deal.
>
> DOUGLAS LARSON

Wayne Herkal (RHS '57) and I burned down a chunk of the big woods while playing with farmer matches. For once we weren't able to stomp out one of the small fires we liked to start. Wayne fled, scared, toward the river. I ran home, trying to keep from thinking about what we had just done. Once safely in my house, I lifted up one of the wooden slats of the Venetian blinds on the dining room window and peeked out just as the fire engines roared past. I died a little.

About ten minutes later, I screwed up my courage and went back down to the edge of the woods, the scene of my crime. I walked up to some onlookers standing across the street.

"Gee, what happened?"

"One of the biggest fires in years. It came all the way up here to the fence."

"Wow!"

"Yeah. Almost to the edge of Michael Dowling School over there," a voice piped up, pointing to a set of buildings down on River Road.

I didn't tell anyone, not even my brother. I think I mentioned it when I went to confession that next Saturday. But I didn't give much detail.

There were a lot of things we didn't tell our parents back then, some minor, some not so.

> I put on lipstick on my way to Nokomis Junior High and wiped it off on the way home. Nice girls did not wear lipstick.
>
> RUTH JOHNSON

> Eddy Schuck, Donald Erickson, Peter Dobratz and I would walk up the storm sewer next to the Nokomis Avenue bridge over the creek. Stooping over, we got as far as 45th Street to look up through the sewer grate. There was another sewer next to the 34th Avenue creek bridge that was a little smaller. For that one we would have to crawl. We got under the parkway to look up that grate.
>
> PAUL GORGOS

The dumbest thing I have ever done — EVER! I was in ninth grade. (It was the railroad trestle bridge over the Mississippi.) Getting across was horrific, only a guardrail to hold onto for dear life, and hold it even tighter when the train came along. I was the only one who didn't go back the same way. I got smart and walked back across on the Lake Street Bridge.

JUDITH SLAVIK

One summer at Lake Nokomis, when I was twelve years old, I jumped off the high tower at Big Beach.

JORUN OLSON

I got kicked out of Lutheran confirmation class for being "restless and goofing off, singing, talking to the other kids in class, etc. A regular pest." After wondering to myself, "Who does he think he is, kicking me out?" I vowed to get back at him and take care of things. I spent an entire week alternately weeping for my soul and crying out/ cursing my bad luck. I was going to be a family disgrace. My mother was probably going to be admitted, with a broken heart, to an asylum. My dad would forever be at the bar telling the world about his dumb kid. Finally, I sucked up my fear, took critical measure of the world around me and "grew up" a whole bunch (without realizing it). I called the confirmation teacher, asking if I could see him and talk about my predicament. He agreed to a visit, so I called on him. I apologized, begged forgiveness, prayed for compassion, promised to behave, ALWAYS, in his class (and everywhere else). He accepted me back in class. Did I ever tell my mother and dad? Heck no! I have never told anybody. Nobody! (Except now, my former classmates.)

CHARLES GUDMUNSON

I acted as lookout when I went with my brothers and their best friend down to the Ford bridge and the three of them would crawl across the arches. I was there as their witness in case one of them fell, so I could go get help. (Of course they would be dead, so I guess I was there to call the mortuary.) I think they finally told their mothers, after they were much older, but I was sworn to silence.

GLORIA BLUMKE

6

The Plymouth–E. 25th Street streetcar — cowcatcher on the front — had turned the corner at 46th and was coming toward us. The tracks in front of us began to vibrate, then we heard a heavy, steel on steel, rolling sound. A loud hiss followed a high-pitched screeching. The brakes were taking hold. The car stopped in front of us and the door folded open.

It was in the early '40s when I became aware that my father and grandfather wore the same uniform to work. They were both motormen for the streetcars (trolleys) operated by the Twin City Lines. As time progressed, my grandfather ended up being a conductor, collecting fares at the back of the streetcar. Only the busy routes had them. I remember riding the Selby–Lake line when my father was the motorman and my grandfather was the conductor. When my father drove the Plymouth–E. 25th line, I would jump on at 46th and 46th, and ride with him to St. Paul and back. On July 10, 1953, the last trolley ran on the Selby–Lake line. My father was one of the last to operate a trolley that day on the line.

JAMES C. MEYERS

Streetcars and bikes were our source of transportation. Joe Smith and I took the streetcar downtown starting when we were eight years old. Once someone dared me to hang by the streetcar strap all the way home and I did. My older brother and I often went to the downtown YMCA to swim, followed by baked beans and a cherry Coke at the Dayton's lunch counter. Then home again on the streetcar.

TOM STACY

Gilbert C. Meyers (father of James C.) on his Selby – Lake route. Courtesy James C. Myers.

My father drove one of those — the one that went out on that old bridge by Fort Snelling. We used to get on at 50th Street and 42nd Avenue and ride with him. We would bring him his lunch and then ride back downtown, and then finally return to our corner. Great memories of another time!

GLORIA BLUMKE

I stepped up and put a token into the smooth, worn-down slot in the brass-plated box. Then ran over and sat on one of the slippery woven cane seats — so hot in the summer — and slid over to the open window. I leaned my elbows on the sill, looking out. Bobby stayed back, crowding the motorman, waiting for him to use his free hand to twirl the knob that mixed the tokens in the little glass case — *ka-ching, ka-ching.*

Streetcar interior (looking toward front and motorman's seat).
Courtesy James C. Myers.

I waved to Dickie, who was slowly walking along the curbing across from the Mobil Gas filling station with the "flying red horse" sign on the roof. His head was down, looking for butts along the gutter. He liked the half-smoked ones — "longies" — good enough to smoke.

A grown-up sitting behind me asked the usual question. I ignored him. He asked it again. I finally turned around and said, "No, I don't know." An older boy on our block told me once that when they asked where I got my freckles and red hair, I should say to them, "from the milkman." I didn't know what he meant by that.

We slowed down and stopped, ready to turn north at Holm Drugstore on 42nd. Dickie must have quit his butt collecting, because I looked out the back window and saw him come running up behind the streetcar. Someone must have double-dared him to do it, because just then he jumped up on the rear of the streetcar and yanked the connector pole and wheel off the overhead cable. We stopped. The motorman bolted from his seat, down and out the door, back alongside our stalled streetcar, cursing at no one in particular. Dickie had disappeared back down the alley. The motorman nestled the pole and its wheel back onto the overhead cable, and we went on.

As we turned the corner, I crossed the aisle over to an open window and waved to Bud Black's older brother Bill (RHS '49) pumping gas at the filling station on the corner. The streetcar headed north toward the bus line on 38th Street when we passed the paper shack where John Pollard and I folded papers for our early-morning routes. A lot of future classmates had such entry-level money-making ventures. They folded *Tribune* editions on the same dark mornings in other neighborhood shacks — Jimmy Carlson down on Lake Street, and Joe Steiner and Dave Gilman at their shack on 38th Street, between Cedar and 18th. Those were our first money-making ventures.

Shoveling snow in winter could bring in heavy money, and so could cutting grass in summer. We also experimented with commerce in the form of Kool-Aid stands, though this rarely brought in much. While I did all this, my first contractual work came at about the age of ten, when I delivered a local shopping newspaper for about $1 per week.

RONALD PETERSON

A few years earlier, I had a small-kid job. A playmate and I had a lemonade stand at the streetcar stop at the end of my block. We did OK, but I was always nervous making change with a customer staring down at me. (For that very reason, I would be dismissed a few years later as homeroom treasurer when I didn't do a very good job keeping track of the money I had collected for a class picnic.)

Still others thought a career in show business might be a path to riches.

I remember putting on shows that would include my friend Peggy Smith, a year younger than me, her sister Julie, and my sister Kris. We used the Smiths' one-car garage on the alley because they had a concrete driveway where the audience — younger kids in the neighborhood — could sit comfortably. Also, they lived on the corner, so sometimes we'd get people from other neighborhoods. Our driveway was gravel, so not so good. Peggy and I always had the lead roles, since we were older. We'd usually sing and dance. I remember singing "I'm looking over a four-leaf clover…." That and many of Patti Page's songs and some silly ones, like "Abba dabba dabba said the monkey to the chimp." We'd make some Kool-Aid, and Peggy's mom would make popcorn. We'd charge the kids who came a dime if they wanted the whole package or a nickel if they just wanted to watch the show. I think most enjoyed the snacks more than the show. We probably only made enough money to buy the Kool-Aid for the next production.

JORUN OLSON

But when they confronted a flurry of mixed reviews and dwindling box-office receipts, the kid producers held a final curtain call and went on to more promising money-making ventures.

A more lucrative way of making money was to collect empty pop bottles scattered around Lake Nokomis. There weren't many trash cans around, except at the beaches, and no fines for littering, so we could easily make a few dollars by returning the bottles to the drug store. If I was saving up for something, like a game or piece of jewelry, I could send away for something from a comic book ad. I'd check around the pathway by the lake every day, especially on Mondays. But quite often we'd just spend our cash on a cherry Coke up at the drugstore.

JORUN OLSON

The two girls had competition on those Monday mornings.

We would go around Nokomis on Mondays to collect
pop bottles to trade in for two cents apiece. Then go play
miniature golf.

DOUGLAS LARSON

Some entered the world of commerce at even earlier years,
age being no impediment to youthful entrepreneurial start-ups.

In my pre-K summer, a friend and I would walk our
alley and go door to door trying to sell small pieces of
concrete, and it worked. This same friend and I would
entertain neighbors along the alley with singing. They
gave us pennies!

ARLOINE HULLAR

7

We came up to 38th Street, across from the newly built
Riverview movie theater, the 1948 successor to the Falls. While
it was an upgrade from the old one up on Minnehaha, I was
still fond of my first theater, where the lobby always smelled of
popcorn, the regular kind only (the more expensive, new and
improved, buttered kind came later when the Riverview opened).
At the Falls, once the house lights went out a Movietone Newsreel opened with a bunch of gymnasts in their underwear vault-
ing over a piece of furniture set out in a schoolyard. Then an
announcer with the "Voice of God" came on with the news. He
told us that the "Red Tide of Communism" was advancing all
over Europe and Asia. It was 1947.

After the cartoons, the serials came on. They were thrillers.
We found ourselves helpless and fear-stricken. We'd grip the
armrest and kick at the back of the seat in front of us in an effort
to help out whoever was in distress — at the edge of a cliff or a
waterfall, or trapped in a cave a few feet from an entrance guarded by a coiling cobra — all with little chance of survival or escape.

But at the very worst moment of stress and fright, the
house lights came on. We would be told to return next Saturday
to view the climactic end of the drama. With an eight-year-old's
boundless optimism, we came back the next week and slid another twelve cents through the slot of the ticket window to the nice
lady who sat behind the glass. We were determined to witness

happy endings. And all of them were. But we found our heroes, once again, in peril — just as the house lights came on.

Those same serials ran at other neighborhoods theaters — the Avalon, El Lago, Nile, Leola and Parkway.

Hopalong Cassidy gave us hope each Saturday. After he held off the bad guys — Black Bart and his gang — the lights came back on and we piled out onto the street, passing a glass-encased glossy of Henry Fonda next to a billboard telling us that *My Darling Clementine* would be coming the next week.

> My sisters and I also went to the movies whenever we got a quarter from parents. We had two choices — the Nile, which we had to take the streetcar to, and the Leola, which we could walk to. Saturdays were a mob scene, but we loved it.
>
> JUDITH KIBBY

> An allowance first, at least for me, consisted of $0.25 weekly. This was enough for a movie at the Nile Theater ($0.12), popcorn ($0.10) and a residue of three cents to splurge on whatever we wanted.
>
> RONALD PETERSON

> Around the time I was 11 or 12, my mother taught me how to use public transportation. On Saturday mornings, my younger sister and I, and usually a few friends, took the shuttle, transferred to the streetcar and went to the

Saturday matinee at the Parkway Theater on 48th and Chicago. The feature was often an exciting serial with a "cliffhanger" to keep us coming back each week. One of my favorites was *Tarzan*. We'd spend many hours back at home climbing trees and trying to swing from limb-to-limb.

JORUN OLSON

The Leola Theater was another hangout. Every Saturday, we would watch the matinee movie, then play the main characters of the movie on the way home.

DOUGLAS LARSON

Sometimes the movie moments were pretty scary. I insisted that my brother flee the theater with me during a showing at the Falls of Agatha Christie's murder mystery *And Then There Were None* (aka *Ten Little Indians*).

The scariest thing happened in an alley when I was eight years old. We saw the scariest movie ever — *Frankenstein*. Well, the next night we were walking through the alley on our way home, and about three garages away we heard this noise. Out from behind that garage came this big older kid walking and making noises like Frankenstein. Well, he scared the living wits out of us, and we didn't walk through any alleys at night for some time after that.

JOSEPH STEINER

Some time around seventh or eighth grade, a movie came out that was called *The Thing*. I was never one who liked ghost stories or science-fiction horror flicks, and I had heard that *The Thing* was very realistic and could scare the fire out of a guy. I held back. But I was challenged, of course, and did not want to be the wimp, so I agreed to go to the Nile with a small group of nervous Folwell guys. The movie was a science-fiction flick — details long forgotten. At the end, however, this "Thing" was in a lab/warehouse/cave (whatever) attacking the humans, snatching them up one by one, as I recall. (Fuzzy recall, I'd guess.) It was gruesome. Abruptly, the movie was over — no elimination of the "Monster," no real conclusion. Like, maybe "The Thing" was still out there waiting for me. Holy Cow! Like, maybe out behind the theater? It scared me SO dang bad! So, unpredictably and abruptly, I slammed out the front door of the Nile and began running, full speed, up the very middle of 23rd Avenue, past Jeanett Pfeifer's, past Greg Larson's, all the way to 35th Street, looking for something (ANYTHING!) with traffic on it; I was afraid to go down a dark side street or alley. I still remember — *The Thing*!

Charles Gudmunson

My mom wouldn't let me see *The Thing*.

The Riverview gave us a modern movie-watching experience (and buttered popcorn). That Movietone Newsreel guy with the

"Voice" appeared again — backed up by inspirational marching music in the background — to tell how our troops held off an all-out North Korean offensive. He also mentioned that an American named George Jorgensen went off to Denmark and came back a woman by the name of Christine Jorgensen. We had trouble with that news item.

A year or so later, we stopped going to movies just with guys.

John Pollard and I had our first movie dates at the Riverview. We came down by streetcar to get ahead of them — Arloine Dolan and Carol Pete. They walked down 42nd. We saw them outside, through the glass-walled lobby at the ticket window. Our plan worked — to meet them inside so we wouldn't have to buy their tickets. But I did share my Milk Duds with Arloine. The movie was *Kim*, with Dean Stockwell and Errol Flynn.

About that time I saw a newsreel that showed that we had dropped a hydrogen bomb over some island in the Pacific Ocean. That was scary. It made a lot bigger mushroom than the ones we dropped on the Japs. Maybe we did it to scare the North Koreans and the Red Chinese. I knew that in a few years I'd be old enough to fight them. I wanted to fly a Sabre jet and shoot down commie MIGs. Then I'd come home and they'd have a parade right down 42nd for me and my new bride, Arloine.

But in the meantime, kid-movie dates continued; sometimes the boy even paid for the girl's ticket (as well as the Milk Duds).

After knowing Ann through all of sixth grade, I asked her to a movie at the Avalon Theater at Bloomington and

Lake Street. I saved the money, and we walked the five blocks to the Bloomington streetcar line and went to Lake Street. I don't recall the movie, but I felt so grown up — a first date, my own money. Wow!

PAUL WULKAN

My first movie date was in the fifth grade; his name was Dale. His mother called my mother on the phone and asked if it was all right if her son took me to the movies on Saturday. I got all dressed up in my Sunday best, and he and I walked three blocks to the El Lago Theater, and he bought our tickets. He didn't put his arm around me or try to kiss me — but then we had run into another guy from school who decided he would join us, so it ended up a threesome (not very romantic), and they both walked me home.

MARLYS OLSON

And yet some girls wanted the independence of paying their own way.

Yes, a movie date at the Leola Theater for an afternoon movie! We met there. I walked and think he did too, but don't know where he lived. Of course, I paid my own way. Didn't know there could be any other way. Don't have a clue what we saw. Yes, *I saw every moment!* Arm moved around my shoulders, but no smooch or anything else. I can "see" him but can't come up with his name. Shorter than I for sure! I was five-foot-seven. Only the one "date," but my heart was all atwitter.

ARLOINE HULLAR

I was a monk in the early years and would not have participated in such a depraved activity. Before high-school? (P.S., I later threw off the orders!)

RONALD PETERSON

At times there was safety in numbers.

At about seven or eight years old, our grade-school group would meet our dates in the Leola theater — 12 cents for a Saturday matinee — then sit with our dates. My date was Carol Hanson (RHS '57). Movie was likely Roy Rogers and, of course, the serial. Walked six blocks to the theater.

JOHN HRKAL

I don't remember taking a girl to a movie until "much" later in life. Could be I was apprehensive about what might take place. Y'see, I was an usher at the Nile Theater for a few months when I was about 15. Got to wear that absolutely stunning two-tone green uniform (with white shirt and tie) and attempted to keep order and civility in the women's lounge and bathroom. I was also charged with keeping an eye on the Amorous Ones seated way in the back, to see that things did not get out of hand. The "wrestling" was easily as volatile and quick as anything from the WWF [World Wrestling Federation]. Luckily for all concerned, I never had to respond to a cry for help, and I never shined my flashlight on the "activity." No need to get punched, eh?

CHARLES GUDMUNSON

Some waited for the *Creature from the Black Lagoon* to come to their local theater so they could put their arm around a frightened date. And then some waited even later.

I did not have a real date until I was a senior.[9] Certainly not in junior high. We went to a movie at the Radio City Theater in downtown Minneapolis. I drove my dad's '54 Buick Special. I can't remember the movie. We may have stopped somewhere on the way home for a Coke after but I'm not sure.

PAUL GORGOS

---

[9]Understandable. In his senior year in high school, Paul appeared in the yearbook as one of the "Top Teddies" for 1957 under the category of "Shyest."

8

As the streetcar crossed the intersection, we were surprised to see a crowd in front of Crane's Drug Store. We looked again and saw that it was an outdoor yo-yo demonstration by a visiting Duncan guy. As we passed, he was showing the crowd how to "walk the dog" and "rock the cradle." One of the prizes to a contestant was a yo-yo with rhinestone studs.

The corner would become a hangout next year for three wanna-be bullies in their brown leather jackets, with lead weights inside their gloves, molded to fit inside a fist. They picked fights at random. One of them was a schoolboy — award-winning accordionist by day, a thug by night. Another had graduated from playground fights in grade school to drugstore corner fights and was well on his way to the bar parking lot fights down on Riverside.

There were other drugstore corners across the neighborhoods that served the needs of stand-around (or sit-inside) teenagers, but they weren't venues for fights.

> The soda fountain was a long, flat, marble-like counter, from which were dispensed a thrilling variety of frozen concoctions — ice cream sodas, sundaes, banana splits — and soft drinks like root beer, cherry Coke, cherry phosphate, lemon and lime, and regular Coke. The soft drinks were made up special. The flavored syrup was poured into the glass and then fizzed up with carbonated water

from a pressurized hose. The young man who worked at the soda fountain was called a soda jerk. My brother Roger wanted to be a soda jerk when he grew up.

RUTH JOHNSON

We approached my soon-to-be junior high school. I didn't know that a year later I would hear about Bruce and Janice. I looked up at a second-floor window, the room where Ms. Motes taught. Bruce had her for World History I.

I never anticipated the "Romeo and Juliet" scenes that played out in the hallways and lunchrooms of eighth and ninth grade Sanford — likely, Folwell and Nokomis as well — when boys and girls discovered each other.

Janice, a love-struck eighth-grade "Juliet" sent Carol, her best friend, on an errand of the heart over to an eighth-grade boy in the lunchroom with the simple question, "Bruce…Janice wants to like you, do you want to like her?"

Bruce, a budding "Romeo," remembered the day before, when Janice had looked back at him and smiled as she was leaving the lunchroom. From that moment, he knew they would be friends for life. He smiled and answered Carol, "Yes."

Cupid's arrows started flying that night. Janice, in the privacy of her room and atop a bed that she shared with two huge fluffy rabbits, wrote a note (in beautiful Palmer Method penmanship) pledging her "everlasting love" for Bruce. She included a lipstick smack at the bottom of it and sprinkled some perfume ("Heavenly Nites") on the envelope that she had spied earlier that day under the glass cosmetics case at Crane's.

Carol passed the note to Bruce the next morning in the hallway as he was moving from his homeroom to Miss Motes' World History I class. He was so distracted that he forgot to write down that "modern civilization began in the Tigris-Euphrates Valley."

But, alas! The "everlasting" lasted for only two weeks when Bruce saw Janice at a Riverview Saturday matinee, a ninth grader's arm around her just before they turned the house lights out.

Bruce was crushed. He hadn't even gotten into the game of girlfriend-boyfriend swaps. He was just dumped — a real surprise, given his popularity in the hallways.

Swapping was a customary practice with junior-high romances, like trading partners on the dance floor. Most alliances were short lived, and couples exchanged partners after "going steady" for at least four weeks or three movies, whichever came first. If it wasn't a boyfriend-girlfriend trade, that is, even-up, and one person got dumped as was Bruce, word got out the next morning that the just-broken heart was available. He was back in the pool.

However, some of the breakups were hard on the former "lovers." For distraction, the boys often took to sports, the girls to cherry vanilla ice cream.

Other eighth graders were not interested in the hallway note-passing games, for various reasons. Some thought, "All that stuff can come later." Others had misgivings about themselves when approaching the opposite sex. Many didn't have the self assurance that Janice and Bruce had. It had a lot to do with self-esteem, the kind that Bruce and his pals had as they walked the hallways of their junior high schools with Brylcreem's "a little dab'll do ya!" peacock confidence, and a whiff of Old Spice trailing behind them.

Eighth grade, Nokomis (Mrs. Bay's homeroom). **Front row:** *Lynette Larson, Judy Adler, Kay Morgan, Ron Kahlman, John Elliott, Steve Nelson, Ron Eikaas.* **Second row:** *Neil (Buddy) Berg, Roger Larson, Tom Price, Dale McDowell, Doug Mohl, (unknown), Alan Gross.* **Third row:** *Carolyn Jardine, Jeraldine Wold, Barbara Goranson, Nelphia Buss, Nancy Peterson, Jerry Stein, Jerry Carlson, Darrel Severson, Buddy Berg.* **Back row:** *Lynnette Morriem, Colleen Canniff, Jorun Olson, Diane Schumacher, Eva Tourtelotte, Carolyn Cecka, Mary Beth Patterson, Faith Benson. Courtesy Jorun (Olson) Robillard.*

A "boy/girl" party of eighth graders St. Helena Catholic School (1953). **Front row:** *James Johnson (partially hidden), Thomas Reiter, Eugene Grazzini, Edward Fleetham, William Berger, Richard Wortman, George Jansen.* **Second row:** *Geraldine Bingham, Mary Ellen Wiencke.* **Back row:** *Mary Murphy (partially hidden), Suzanne Frederick, Mary Ellen Woodfill, Judith Newfield, Carol Knapp, Mary Ellen McManus, Mary Ruth Lucey, Mary Margaret Hanson. Courtesy Geraldine Bingham.*

Peer acceptance in junior high, for many, was as important as a good grade in algebra or physical science class.

As an overweight kid, I was bullied by my classmates in many ways. One class that was really hard was gym. Never got picked for a team, so the teacher would put me on one of her choosing, much to the dislike of that team. They would say disgusting things and everyone had a good laugh at my expense. I didn't really have any friends in grade school. Later, in junior high, I began to be a little more acceptable and slimmed down some, but those years were hard for most kids. Either you had to be very smart, and of course really good looking, or it was hard to fit in. Those years, my defense was to be as funny as I could be. That remained my way of making friends.[10] I tried not to hurt feelings or make them mad, just laugh with me. Seems those young years shaped most of who we are today.

JUDITH KIBBY

[I was shy] with a red face most of my school days. They would call my name for current events. I was ready but said, "Nope, not ready." And the times I had the courage to raise my hand I was relieved when the teacher called on another raised hand.

JEANETT PFEIFER

---

[10]And that way worked. In her senior year of high school, Judy appeared in the yearbook as one of the "Top Teddies" for 1957 under the category of "Wittiest."

I was small but not skinny. I remember a summer day at Little Beach when a boy in our class called me "Crisco." In other words, "fat in the can." I was mortified. I told him about it at our 50th reunion. But it just shows you how words can be hurtful. I still remember it from God knows how many years later.

GERALDINE BINGHAM

Passing notes to boys was too scary — at least for me. I was very unsure of myself those years, skinny thing I was. Very comfortable with my many girlfriends, but not with boys.

JOANNE MAHRE

Folwell girls in their "DuShons" outfits.
Joanne Mahre, Janel Scriven, Val Harrington.
Courtesy Joanne (Mahre) Haugen.

In an attempt to narrow the knowledge-about-each-other gap that existed between junior-high boys and girls, and to do it in a constructive and responsible way, parents and neighborhood leaders organized dance nights for the students.

I'm not sure what the other schools did, but at Nokomis Junior High the Friday-night canteen dance was the big thing — especially for most of the girls. It was once a month on Friday nights. The girls lined up on one side of the gym and the boys on the opposite side. The early dancers on the floor were generally a few girls dancing with each other. Then it was Bruce Bergman and a partner doing a type of polka. He and his partners were really good. Then a few ninth-grade couples joined in but most of us guys stood along the wall with the hanging mats and just talked. Most of us felt that it was an accomplishment if we danced maybe two times. The dances were organized and run by the parents and not the school.

THOMAS STACY

There wasn't a whole lot of dancing at Nokomis that went on, but we did have fun getting together.

DOUGLAS LARSON

The pastor's wife at my church, Nokomis Lutheran, didn't approve of dancing and was always trying to get the dances changed to square dances.

THOMAS STACY

Ah! Square dancing (read: hand to hand with an occasional waist turn). While the pastor's wife didn't get her wish, she probably didn't object to Lutheran-with-Lutheran dancing. She might've raised her eyebrow a bit if a Baptist or Methodist had cut in. Had a Catholic boy done so, however, someone would've had to run for the school nurse to revive the "woman who had just fainted on the gymnasium floor."

Dancing royalty. Queen Gerry Bingham and King Doug Larson (1954). Courtesy Gerry Bingham.

Church and state issues never clashed at the neighborhood "crepe paper and low-light" evenings over at Sibley. There were no constraints on teenage discovery as the dancing was slow (read: body-to-body, full-frontal).

Sibley was two short blocks from my home, so we spent a lot of time there as striplings, both winter and summer. The main building was the scene of our first dances and our chance to hold a girl for a minute or two.

RONALD PETERSON

I remember dancing on Thursday and Friday nights in junior high. We danced with girls, as very few boys could dance.

JEANETT PFEIFER

Sibley Field House had dances on Thursday nights, which made an impression on me because my parents were in charge when I was a ninth grader. The park would decorate the main room with crepe paper, lower the lights and play the music of the day. I was dressed in a sport coat and a tie, after my mother's inspection. We knew that dancing with live girls was some sort of major life achievement. This was the start of our introduction to adulthood. We would bring along aspirin, as the legend had it that Coke and aspirin would cause arousal — like a 14-year-old would need it. Yes, we would sometimes even get aroused enough to press ourselves against the girl. Lots of times they would not even pull away. What a glorious world did Sibley Park provide!

PAUL WULKAN

I wasn't supposed to go to the dances at Sibley, but would stay overnight at a friend's and thus be able to go without my parents knowing. That's about as "rebellious" as it got for me.

JOANNE MAHRE

I think it was in seventh or eighth grade that the Park Board began holding a dance at Sibley, one night a week. For many of us, that spelled the end of our athletic careers (or at least diminished interest on Fridays). There were GIRLS at the park. And there was music, and there were fast dances, and there were slow dances — and it was (as best I can remember) absolutely wonderful that a regular, dumb, small, unimpressive kid could actually put his arm around a cute young lady and move around the floor, pretending to dance. That was some kinda good deal! Brylcreem kept the pompadour in place. Mennen Skin Bracer was, I think, the fragrance of choice at age 13. Probably because it had a pretty stout "manly" smell. We were so incredibly cool! At age 12 or 13 most of us were simply bedazzled — both by the concept AND the action! With little hesitation, I can say that it was kinda like a rite of passage into the young-adult world for many of us ordinary boys.

CHARLES GUDMUNSON

Graduation Day, Nokomis Junior High, 1954.
Seated: *Jim Hovanetz, Steve Nelson, Bill Rataczak.*
Standing: *Jim Keely, Gary Frazier, Doug Larson, Paul Gorgos, Ron Eikaas, Ron Johnson. Courtesy Gerry Bingham.*

Graduation Day, Folwell Junior High, 1954.
Debbie Christensen, Jeanett Pfeifer, Joanne Mahre.
Courtesy Joanne (Mahre) Haugen.

Graduation Day, Sanford Junior High, 1954.
Courtesy Carolann (Hendrix) Lavell.

9

From the streetcar window, I saw a boy enter the alley across from the school, maybe on his way home. He might've been my age. He kept his head down, staring at the concrete, as if looking for something. He reminded me of one of the kids in our grade school.

His name was Donald, a kid who wore the same clothes, day after day, had bad hair and personal hygiene, a slow learner. Come to think of it, he was the one who got just one or two Valentine cards from his classmates in fourth grade. Sad. I doubt if he was anyone's best friend or ever had one, when most of us had two or three of them. I guessed, a childhood filled with sadness and pain.

We knew little about him. He tried to join in on some of the pick-up games over on the playground. He wasn't very athletic, was always chosen last and put in right field. He tried hard. At other times he stood over by the swings. Alone. I think he even felt lonely in a crowd of us kids. Donald never raised his hand in class, never got picked to be on anything, and walked the hallway alone. Often the teacher let him stay in during recess.

He was easy prey for a bully. He could not fend for himself, nor respond to the unthinking kid-meanness of some of his class-mates. No doubt a few of them called him crazy behind his back — and maybe not "behind." Maybe he went down alleys with a kind of a headache-like darkness and confusion that his parents tried to cover up, if they even knew. If they didn't know, how could we?

And others kids must have been troubled. We didn't know that shyness or sulking might have been a result of mental depression, or that their anger came from the mood swings of a bipolar disorder or a manic-depressive condition that they took into their adulthood. All we knew as kids came from overheard adult whispers — about places like St. Peter's, places we kids called "funny farms."

Sometimes the condition didn't show until later years. But who really knew whether or not symptoms surfaced, unnoticed, in kid years?

I grew up in a home with depression (my dad). Years later, I was diagnosed with dysthymia, which is a kind of depression. I had inherited it. I looked back on my junior-high years. I remember looking to the future with uncertainty, if not dread, instead of anticipation. It was hard for me to face new experiences with any joy. I yearned to be like my friends who could. I would sit alone in the cafeteria, because I thought it had something to do with being unpopular. It hurt. I was clueless about clothes and hair. Every once in a while, a popular girl would have pity on me and tell me in a nice way that my black-and-white striped shirt did not go with my red-and-black-plaid skirt. Growing up, I thought that only adults had depression. When our daughter was depressed in fourth grade, I was assured that children do not have depression. Now we know.

RUTH JOHNSON

At that time and age, none of us were able to differentiate between what was normal, abnormal or, sometimes, even bad. I must say that what we now diagnose today we then called a behavioral trait or a pain in the ass. Things that were out of the ordinary and suspect were: bachelors living alone and divorced women. People who went to neighborhood bars were of questionable character. In my neighborhood, we had one of each, but no one bothered anyone. A friend in my neighborhood told me, as an adult, that he (Terry Baxter) was bipolar. I only recall that he was more daring than the other kids, but then most bipolar persons are never diagnosed until about age 45, after they have lost marriages, jobs, income, etc.

PAUL WULKAN

My sister, Janice Olson, RHS class of '54, suffered from bipolar disorder, but it didn't show up (that I'm aware of) until she was an adult. It affected her life to the point where she could not work, although she was college educated and briefly held down some pretty impressive jobs and was a very talented pianist. She simply could not get along with her co-workers (or family, for that matter) because of her mood swings. You never knew who was going to walk through that door. I did not see her for 25 years, although we kept in touch by mail and phone calls, but that was the only way we could have a relationship. It was truly a tragic life. She just passed away this year, a month before her 80th birthday. I spoke to her by phone the day she died. I hope she has finally found peace. The rest of our family is fine. Hopefully this painful and ugly disease will not re-surface in our family again.

MARLYS OLSON

Then there were the kids who were not confused. They knew. Alcohol, with or without the demons of mental disease, fueled the violence in some homes. Tommy, two blocks over, showed up at the swings one Saturday morning and said that the bruises on his face came from a fight with his older brother. Maybe the truth lay elsewhere in his house. We only remember that his mom gave us cookies whenever we went up to the back screen door.

If not violent toward the children at least alcohol fed family dysfunction.

My dad was a full-blown alcoholic. So was my stepmom. When he was dry, for months at a time, he was great. But when he went back to the bottle it was tough to be around him. It was about the time I had my first paper route job. My brother Dick and I started jobs early... maybe I was in sixth grade. I opened a savings account at a bank down on Lake Street. Because I was too young to have one solely in my name, my dad had to cosign for me. He would raid the account from time to time to support his drinking habit.

JAMES CARLSON

In my family, this was never talked about, although in my immediate family there wasn't much drinking. I figured out years later, however, that my maternal grandfather was an alcoholic. I don't even remember a liquor cabinet, but think there were a few bottles in the cupboard. There was a childless couple in the neighborhood who probably hit the bottle a little too much (at least the husband did), but I never had the sense they bothered anyone and no one talked about them, at least that I was aware of.

CYNTHIA KERSTEN

My dad was a handsome, smart, fun guy (star athlete, class president in high school) whose drinking got the best of him. He drank at the bar on his way home from his blue-collar job, but he never drank at home. He was usually a few sheets to the wind by the time he got home and then slept it off on the couch before dinner. Then my mom (a nondrinker) and dad would fight (verbally), usually about the lack of money and, of course, religion (mixed marriage). It bothered me greatly, and I remember being ashamed and embarrassed. I just wanted him to disappear. Alcoholism was not understood during that time. It was considered a weakness and, like everything else in those days, "a sin." I don't think my friends thought of my dad as a drunk. He was a very good guy, but he really wasn't present for me or my sisters during our growing up years. He was in his late 50s when he quit drinking. He was a dedicated member of AA for 17 years before he died and did so much to help others who suffered from alcoholism.

GERALDINE BINGHAM

10

The streetcar passed alongside the field in back of the school and came up to the small grocery store at the next corner, 35th and 42nd. I recognized an older boy — in my brother's class at Sanford — standing up against a wall. He wore a long, dirty white apron. He was on a break. It may have been his first clock-in job.

Those were important for our self-esteem and for "leaving the nest" development.

I first "punched in" at the passenger-terminal restaurant of the old Wold Chamberlain, where I was a busboy. I think I was fourteen. It was my first regular job. I never called caddying a regular job, not when Pollard and I hauled heavy golf bags around Minikahda for the likes of people named Totten P. Heffelfinger. (That name. I always wondered about people who had last names for first names. Maybe it was because they were rich. Or maybe his mother was a "Totten" and wanted equal billing. None of us around the caddy shack had two last names.)

Busboy. It was a man's job; no one ever heard of a "busgirl." I tried to do my best. I remember when a small chartered plane arrived from Chicago with a Canada-bound hunting party. A slick-haired, fast-talking guy off the plane came up to me in the restaurant. He looked dark, maybe Jewish or Italian, not Swedish or Norwegian, which was a big part of my south-side worldview of adults at the time. He asked where he could get a drink. I quickly got him a glass of water. It was a drink. I even put some ice into it. I was happy to help out. He left without touching it.

I would stand at the screen door at the back of the restaurant on my breaks and watch the Stratocruisers land. I remember when our fifth-grade class had a guided trip through one of them. Wow! A spiral staircase inside. I watched with wonder as they took off on "the shortest, fastest route to the Orient." The Orient. The Far East! *Terry and the Pirates*.

It was on those breaks that I could listen to the older guys talk "man talk" as they dragged on their Lucky Strike and Chesterfield cigarettes, knowing that I'd be doing that some day. Yeah, I would plan, in a year or two, to start smoking and be on my way to becoming a real man.

Then a few years later I would plan to go to the Orient on a Stratocruiser and sit in the bar/lounge and have a cocktail and offer a Chesterfield to the pretty girl sitting across from me.

When I was fifteen I worked as a busboy at the Minikahda Club, in Minneapolis, one summer. It was there that I learned how to steal champagne and, once, put on a disastrous show of carting dishes above my head in front of the management.

RONALD PETERSON

My first job was playing the piano for a friend who taught dancing. She was an excellent dancer and taught dancing at a music studio on Nicollet at 16th. The year I was in ninth grade, one day a week after school. It was upstairs, above some store fronts, and was a pretty dark and dingy place. (Later, a dentist who had his office in the same building was accused of raping a patient.[11] Occasionally he would have his door open. His office was across the hall from the music studio, and when I walked by, I could see him working on patients.) I think the thing I liked the most about it, however, was the fact that I was actually earning money. It gave me a real sense of empowerment.

CYNTHIA KERSTEN

My first real job was at Tony Cianciolo's grocery store at the southwest corner of 38th Street and Longfellow Avenue. Tony and his family lived upstairs. My responsibilities included checking the prices at the other grocery store across the street (market research); going with Tony to the old farmers' market downtown to buy produce, flowers, etc.; stocking shelves; wiping off the sausages in the cooler when they started getting a white film; and peeling off lettuce and cabbage leaves and marking the price down when they hadn't sold.

DAVID GILMAN

---

[11] The dentist was the notorious Dr. Arnold Axilrod, who killed his patient, Mary Moonen, in the most sensational (and rare) murder case of our innocent and guarded Minneapolis childhood. The out-of-town tabloids at Shinders' newsstand down on Hennepin carried headlines that screamed, "Minneapolis Dentist Fills Wrong Cavity!"

On the opposite corner (38th and Bloomington) was Silver's Market a small grocery store that provided me with my first employment — shelving stock, sorting pop bottles, burning boxes in the back in a 55-gallon barrel and, best of all, delivering groceries to customers. Sometimes we would do so in Mr. Silver's '35 Dodge truck, but other times in a red wagon or, in the winter, on my sled. I would have to negotiate the snowbanks, with an occasional accident of groceries falling into the snow, which meant wiping the snow from the packages and replacing them in hopes of it being unnoticed. Most pleasant was delivering to nice warm houses and, with luck, getting a nickel tip. I worked there after school and on Saturdays for my $9 weekly check. Wow, real money!

PAUL WULKAN

I started working at Zipp's Pharmacy at age 14 and worked there through high school. Harry Zipperman (the owner and pharmacist) was a good boss who cared about us (my brother and me) and our futures. He encouraged college. I later worked my first year as a dentist over his drugstore.

THOMAS STACY

When I was eleven, my first steady gig came about when I worked in my dad's shop on Saturdays. I could clean up, eviscerate chickens and do other work for a few dollars. I wanted to do this since my dad was, largely, an absent figure, who worked six days a week and, when home, was still away, since he drank heavily. I wanted to be around him since he was my dad. Next, at roughly the same age, I shifted to work for my uncle in the grocery store next door, and here's where I found my work routine and ethic, for the next six years, starting at 50 cents an hour. I liked working in a neighborhood store, since I interacted with adults and appreciated helping them, as well as getting to know them.

RONALD PETERSON

11

The streetcar turned west at 34th Street, passing Longfellow Park on the left.

> Longfellow Park was a block from my house, and I spent a great deal of time there in the winter. I skated from the first ice until it melted. If I didn't skate down the street to the park, I changed into my skates in the warming house. It was a simple wooden structure with benches and cubbyholes for our shoes. We chased each other around the ice, the boys usually grabbing scarves or hats off the girls they liked. We skated after school and after supper. Girls wore figure skates and boys hockey. I don't recall any organized teams.
>
> PAT EIDE

I saw a small crowd gathered over on one of the softball diamonds. Yes, it was. A kid fight. Like the ones we had at Hiawatha. They usually started with, "Oh yeah?" " Yeah!" "Oh yeah? What grade are you in?"

At the call of "Fight! Fight!" everyone nearby, except the girls who continued to ride on the swings, rushed over to form a ring around the fighters. If they were under twelve, they'd fall to the ground into a wrestling lock. If older, they'd remain on their feet, flailing away at each other. It seemed that each had his own handler in his corner, who were often more interested in the fight than the two boys down in the dirt were.

By then Susan Olafsson, the class tattletale, would've jumped off her swing and run into the open door of her classroom to alert her teacher. Moments later, Mrs. Cochran would run out the door, arms in the air, a ruler in one hand, which she would use to strike the butt of the first combatant she reached. Later that day, both fighters would end up clapping blackboard erasers and writing one of those, "I will not…" 100 times essays.

> I don't remember fights at Howe School, but they may have happened without the girls appreciating what was going on.
>
> CYNTHIA KERSTEN

> There were fights occasionally, usually between boys. I never saw girls fight. They didn't occur on the playground but in the street, on the way home. I witnessed one fight and it made my stomach hurt, so I crossed the street to avoid watching it.
>
> PAT EIDE

The day I was going to be clobbered, Ronnie McKeown was new to Bancroft Elementary School but made quite a stir in our class. He seemed to know more and been to places and otherwise accomplished things that were exotic to the rest of us fourth graders. Anyway, Ronnie and I got into an altercation, which resulted in our deciding to fight it out at noontime. It wasn't my idea, since I was convinced he could beat me to a pulp. Anyway, on a winter's day, coming back from home and lunch, the site of the fight was selected as a stair landing outside Bancroft. I dawdled coming back, hoping to be late and therefore missing the time and site of my near extinction. A couple of the kids who were to be the spectators came out to find me and hurry me along for the execution. A ring of our peers formed on the landing, and Ronnie and I took center stage. A miracle then occurred. I saw that Ronnie was at least as afraid of me as I was of him! We exchanged a couple of perfunctory blows, and the bell rang to tell us to get inside. That was the end of my fighting career, but it still amazes me that somebody could have been afraid of me.

RONALD PETERSON

12

We took the corner at 36th to go north toward Lake Street.
It was the commercial strip of our greater south Minneapolis
neighborhood — auto parts shops, tool-and-die makers, rug
cleaners, mom-and-pop grocery stores, and car dealers, new and
used. Western Auto, a few doors off the intersection, was where
I bought streamers to fit on my bike handles.

The Selby–Lake streetcar line ran east and west along this
street. We didn't take one east very often, over the bridge to St.
Paul. Maybe once a year to the State Fair or the zoo at Como Park.
They called us the "Twin Cities," but we seldom visited our twin.
I guess that's what rivers did.

A friend and I took the streetcar to the State Fair. The fair
was way over in St. Paul, so the trip required two fares —
one for each city. We had to transfer two times, and we
thought we had carefully calibrated how much money
we would need in order to get home. But we'd forgotten
about the two fares. So when the streetcar crossed the
Lake Street Bridge back into Minneapolis and the conductor came around for the additional fare, we had to
admit that we had no money. To his credit he allowed us
to remain on the streetcar, and we were able to continue
riding to our transfer point. I'm not sure what else he
could have done. We were probably eleven years old.

CYNTHIA KERSTEN

Freeman's, the first department store of our childhood, was farther west, at 27th. Families went there when they ran out of hand-me-downs for their kids to wear — or for something special to graduate in. To wear store-bought clothes — not just the homemade ones sewn together from patterns and fabric purchased from neighborhood dry-goods stores (or at Amluxen's downtown) — was a step up.

As a small boy I was enchanted by the overhead flying tubes at Freeman's when my mom brought me there. She would buy something and take it over to a saleslady. The magic began shortly after she handed the woman the money. I held her hand a little tighter when a little cable car whizzed above my head — only minutes later to return from some faraway secret place above the ceiling. I stared up as it stopped right in front of my mom and the store lady. Like a tiny streetcar at a stop. I didn't know what it carried. But my mom did. And so did the lady. Because we always left the store right after that.

> Our dime store did not have cashiers on the sales floor. The cashier was on a mezzanine at the back of the store. The clerk would send our money by pneumatic tube to the cashier, and the cashier would send back change and the receipt. I loved watching that tube.
>
> RUTH JOHNSON

I was also intrigued when my mom took me and my brother to Freeman's to get fitted for new shoes. It was fun stepping up to that tall machine to look down at the green glow of X-rayed bones of our feet in the shoes — wiggle our toes — to make sure they fit. Cynthia Kersten did it there, too. Dave Gilman did his toe-wiggling at Roberts Shoes farther west on Lake at Chicago.

Looking north on Chicago at Lake Street. Note Dave Gilman's Roberts Shoe Store. Photo: Minnesota Historical Society.

The Federated School of Music was around the corner and upstairs on 27th. That's where John Pollard and I started, and ended, our musical careers. Clarinets — my older brother had a wooden one, and mine was metal with dents.

The third-floor hallway was filled with irritating, wheezing and screeching sounds of accordions that drowned out any competing squeals coming from the reed instruments one flight up.

I used the shuttle/streetcar system, lugging my accordion to and from lessons at a studio on Lake Street. The accordion probably weighed nearly as much as I did. It didn't take long for me to decide to forget the accordion.

JORUN OLSON

I took lessons in the fifth and sixth grades, quit but went back in eighth grade. Even got into the senior accordion band. I took the Minnehaha streetcar to 27th & Lake but didn't have to bring my accordion. Started with a 12 base and, of course, they sold us a 120 base after the first 24 lessons. I enjoyed it for quite a while but then practicing interfered with other things in life.

CAROL PETERSON

The Federation people put on a concert each year. The same accordion sounds, by then more in harmony, were heard on the stage at South High on recital night, curtain rising after curtain rising. There was a huge sigh of relief when it finally rose to reveal John, me and fellow band members assembled onstage. George Klemma's *Flight of the Bumblebee* on the clarinet brought the house down. His solo kept the dads, who otherwise would've fled to the hallway for their third cigarette of the night, in their seats. Moms cringed in their seats, wondering if the money set aside for music lessons might have been better spent on a car trip to the Black Hills.

About that time I was convinced that, while half of the south Minneapolis kids were playing kick the can, the other half were taking accordion lessons.

But there were some exceptions.

> I took piano lessons every Thursday at our house. I hated the lessons so would go to the park, Longfellow, instead. The piano teacher, Mr. Johnson, would come looking for me and bring me home in his car. Now, of course, I wish I had taken more interest in it, as I love piano music.
>
> MARLYS OLSON

It was on that same block, Woolworth's on one side and Kresge's across the street, that one of our group began his petty-crime habit. He started out by engaging in what the juvenile-court prosecutors downtown called "third degree retail fraud" (read, shoplifting). I called him "The Whistler," a tag he resented. Every time he was about to make a "hit" on one of the open trays on the display tables, he would start to whistle, feigning nonchalance. As if a veteran sales clerk would confuse that with the time-honored signal of a nervous swiper. But I don't recall that he ever got caught. A few summers later, he beat a path over to Little Beach to join a handful of others in going after more lucrative pickings.

Some started their criminal ways even earlier.

My mother was horrified when I (three or four years old) brought home a lovely bouquet of tulips. I had picked them from Mrs. Jarnberg's garden. As I remember it, Mrs. Jarnberg was very nice about the whole thing.

RUTH JOHNSON

There was a small corner grocery store on 50th Street and 29th or 30th Avenue. What I remember about that store was a big bin of loose peanuts in the shell. I was probably five or six years old, shopping with my dad on a Saturday morning, when he noticed me eating some peanuts. He made me return them and promptly gave me a good lecture about the evils of stealing. I remember that experience to this day.

PAUL GORGOS

When I was caught "red-handed," I was probably ten or so. The store was a local five-and-dime located on 50th Street and 34th Avenue, next to the Leola Theater. I had pulled the old "grab three, pay for two" ploy—packs of gum. When I went to check out with my haul, some kind of manager nailed me with the extra pack in my pocket. He obviously was lying in wait, because I did have fast fingers—at least I thought so. He escorted me downstairs to a damp basement storeroom and sat me down in a dining-room-like chair. My mind was paralyzed, fearing a one-way bus ride to Red Wing, and lost friends. Under the glow of a single low-hanging light bulb, he subjected me to a "Young man I'm gonna call your mom" grilling. Well, there was no phone call, but I missed the serials with my pals that morning. But, more importantly, he did alter my introduction to a possible life of crime, for which I probably should have thanked him. I've been "clean" ever since.

DOUGLAS LARSON

One narrow escape from trouble came when a friend (Judy Kibby) and I noticed a truck dropping off bundles of newspapers for paper carriers (usually kids twelve to fourteen years old) to deliver. They were carefully placed inside people's doors or in their milk boxes. This truck followed pretty much the same route we took walking home from Nokomis Junior High. It seemed like a great idea to sneak into the back of the truck when it made a stop, hide behind bundles of newspapers inside, and hitch a ride as close as possible to our homes. Not smart. It didn't take long before we were discovered and we ended up running blocks out of our way, hiding in between garages and garbage cans in the alleys, scared to death. Never tried that again.

JORUN OLSON

13

We passed by the Canada Dry bottling plant on the left, up on a little grassy hill across from Brackett Field. St. Albert the Great Catholic Church, was a few blocks west. It was the next one north of my St. Helena, well beyond a stone's throw. Distance was not a factor with the profusion of Protestant churches on our neighborhood blocks. (Whose names always seemed to contain the words Nokomis or Minnehaha as often as the word Saint.) A stone's thrown from any one of them was never beyond the next one and surely would have broken a few windows.

Minnesota, the land of multi-ethnics and multi-faiths, might not have been as "multi" in south Minneapolis as it was elsewhere in the state. As far as bragging rights, the Lutherans were the main church-going bloc in my Norsk and Svensk neighborhood. The other Protestant denominations were Baptists, Methodists, and Presbyterians. Catholics were lightly sprinkled among them. There were probably a few Episcopalians. But I heard they had money and lived in big houses over by the lakes.

I didn't know of any Jewish people on our blocks. They were mostly on the north side of the city. Nor did I know much about their religion, although one kid across the street and down said that the Jews had killed Christ — at least that's what his dad had told him.

We Catholic kids were clueless about the other religions. The autocratic pastor at St. Helena made sure we remained so.

We'd be thrown out of the church if we so much as attended a wedding, baptism, or any other service at a non-Catholic church. For the gullible eleven-year-old I once was, that meant that when I walked by Minnehaha Lutheran, if I so much as took a peek inside the big front door, I'd be sent into eternal damnation. That was a lot more serious than peeking into the Hillside Inn, a 3.2 beer place around the corner on 42nd.

But some of the more curious on the Lutheran side wanted to find out what that "other" religion was all about. They risked more than a "peek inside the front door" of a Catholic church.

My circle of friends didn't include many Catholics, so we were rather curious about the rumors of their religion — confession, mandatory attendance, no meat on Fridays, etc. At that time, we were told non-Catholics were not welcome in their churches and practicing Catholics were not allowed to attend anything Protestant, including weddings and funerals. One day in fifth grade, the neighborhood girls plotted to find some kind of scarves or hankies (because we knew enough that it was a sin not to have your head covered) and sneaked into Holy Name. Saw the holy water basin for ourselves, the kneeling benches and — gasp! — the confessional booth, all foreign to us. Then we saw the cross with a figure of Jesus hanging from it. The crucifix. We Lutherans celebrated an empty cross. Christ had risen. We were scared to death we would be caught and suffer some form of punishment, but that didn't happen and we left, giggling, our curiosity satisfied.

JOANNE MAHRE

I attended John Ericcson, and St. Helena's was across the street. Our next-door neighbor kids attended St. Helena's, so I had no real curiosity about it. Nancy went to confession at the church on Saturdays, and periodically, I'd go with her. Of course, I sat in the pew as she went into that cubicle to repent to the priest for all her earthly sins. I could never understand why she had to ask forgiveness from a man vs. my prayers to God! My parents never knew of my "adventures," nor did hers.

ARLOINE HULLAR

When the Catholic students came into the city's public schools in ninth grade, they might have brought better cursive writing and grammar skills, even discipline, but to some, they also brought with them a little bit of the mystery of their religion.

We watched those St. Helena's kids in awe. At the end of recess a nun would come out with a bell and ring it. The kids would quietly line up in front of her for an orderly procession back into the school. We kids ran into the school pell-mell when the outdoor bell rang. No lines. We just went to our desks. What was it like in that school? What were the nuns like? It was a mystery. St. Helena's was a K–8 school, so those kids showed up at Nokomis for ninth grade. We checked them over and talked about them. Well! We were certainly surprised to see them beat us academically, especially in English grammar.

RUTH JOHNSON

Of the Catholic kids in my neighborhood in the late '40s and early '50s, few of us knew about the teachings in the Bible. But there were exceptions.

> When I was in third grade at St. Helena, our Irish pastor, Father Rowan — who scared the bejesus (the Irish expression fits) out of us — offered a challenge to our class. Whoever memorized and recited the 72 books of the Bible (different Bibles have varying numbers of books) would win the grand prize of one dollar. Never mind we didn't actually read or study the Bible. Well, I studied diligently and was successful in my recitation. I thought I had won the lottery. While I no longer have the dollar, I can still recite up to Ecclesiastes!

GERALDINE BINGHAM

Lutherans had summer Bible camps. (Come to think of it, maybe my parents brought me to church one year too early, because when I heard his name during a Lenten service, I thought that Pontius Pilate flew a plane.) But no Bible for us, we were too busy memorizing the Catholic playbook, the dark-brown paperback *Baltimore Catechism*. And memorize we did. By rote, by heart, we memorized. We didn't think.

But I memorized well. One Saturday morning at my confirmation class, I approached our wizened old pastor Fr. Rowan — for all I knew he could've baptized my grandmother as well as my mom — as he sat at a table on a raised platform looking down on us. His gaze struck fear into us, all the way down to our U.S. Keds. (He was slightly deaf, and the deaf often raised their own voices, unwittingly. On Saturday afternoons the lines to his confessional were short. We would hear his scratchy voice from his booth, "How many times?" The poor penitent, probably new to the parish, would sneak out, head down.)

That morning I asked Father Rowan if I could be excused to attend an important baseball game at Sibley. He looked at me, smiled and said he'd release me if I could recite the Eight Beatitudes of Jesus backward. I added that I wanted it to be a package deal and that if I succeeded, Tom Russell (our steady right fielder) got to flee the room as well (not in those exact words). He agreed. So I went back to my seat, set my baseball mitt down on an empty chair and looked up at him. Of course memorizing was all that Catholic kids did in those days. I wondered if I could recite backward what I had memorized forward. I closed my eyes, opened them, and went first to the eighth Beatitude and started working my way back to the front. I did it! Tom and I jumped on our bikes and made it to Sibley in time for the game.

We had some familiarity with the rights and wrongs of the Ten Commandments. We knew the one against stealing, a kid shoplifting. But there were others, like, we should not "covet" a neighbor's wife. That was a bit advanced for me. I didn't even know what "covet" meant. I asked my mom. She didn't give me a very good answer. I also remember reading about the "Seven Deadly Sins." I wouldn't know if I had ever committed something called "sloth."

Beyond memorizing the *Catechism* we were instructed about sins — venial, actual, and the big one, mortal sin. The first two were simple. They were the lesser ones that would not send you to burn in Hell if you committed them, like the mortal one did, unless you repented. Murder was the serious one, like the gangsters on *Boston Blackie* on Saturday nights. If one of them pulled the trigger on someone, he went off to the flames of Hell before the end of the program — no priest in sight.

But I knew that non-Catholics sinned too, that it was a big deal, as anyone would know who passed by the huge Luke Rader billboard down on Lake Street by the bridge over to St. Paul.

In junior high the retreat masters at the Catholic Youth Center down on Park Avenue never mentioned murder. On the other hand, they never mentioned any Christian principles either — compassion, humility, and charity — and not a word about race relations and proper behavior toward the less fortunate human beings among us. No — at the sessions, the priest only railed against the evils of bad thoughts about Girls! Sex! Guilt! If we had improper — the buzzword was "impure" — thoughts about girls' bodies, we'd be sent into eternal damnation unless we got a pass at confession the next Saturday. It was all so confusing. I often wondered how my Lutheran friends got away with bad thoughts about girls' bodies. Maybe for them it wasn't bad if they just didn't go and commit that "covet" thing.

Ah! Confession. To us Catholic kids it was "Get out of jail free." One Lutheran friend remembered thinking as a kid how lucky Catholic kids were because "they could just go to confession and then be free to start all over again. We Lutherans had to think about our guilt a whole lot longer."

I could understand Heaven and Hell, but I had some problems with Heaven's in-between stop, Purgatory. My mom, after mass, would walk up the aisle to the front of the church, off to the left of the communion railing, and kneel at a tray of candles. Some were lighted. She'd light one and pray for deceased relatives, often a great aunt. She'd put some coins through a slot in a metal box. Then we'd leave. She said something about "indulgences" to help Aunt so-and-so get out of Purgatory and on her way to Heaven. I can't remember what she said when I asked about dead aunts from poor families — too poor to put coins into the box. All that was confusing to me, especially when I thought that aunts never got into trouble, particularly "great" ones. Only little boys got into trouble. I was eight or nine years old.

There were few "mixed" marriages (Catholics and Protestants) on our blocks, though some stretched the definition a bit.

Religion was important in our family, even though my parents had a "mixed marriage" — my father was Lutheran and my mother was Methodist. Attending Church every Sunday was just something we did. No discussion. In our public elementary school, kids were released once a week to walk to one of two churches near the school for an hour of catechism. I am thankful for this example of faith and commitment from parents and the community.

JORUN OLSON

And there were moments of humor.

My sisters and I were products of a "mixed marriage." My mother Irish Catholic and my dad Norwegian Lutheran. Truth be told, as kids at St. Helena, the Catholic school we attended, we were a bit embarrassed … that our dad was "non Catholic." So when my sister Barbara was asked by her fourth-grade teacher, Sister Patrick Ann, if her parents would be at her school piano performance, her response was, "My mom will be there but not my dad because he's a Norwegian."

GERALDINE BINGHAM

Anti-Catholic sentiment did not play much of a role in those younger years, surely not on the playground or in the classroom, but in a few instances it surfaced elsewhere.

There were many businessmen, as well as one minister, who did not let their daughters play with any of us, but especially the Catholic kids.

SUSAN CODUTI

However, a few years later…

Religion became more of an issue in high school, when we started to date. God forbid your son or daughter would marry someone of a different religion. Being a product of a "mixed marriage," I knew first-hand the havoc it created in my own parents' marriage. I remember my sister and her high-school boyfriend breaking up because of religious differences. I suppose it was a big deal back then because kids were marrying so young — right out of high school. Thank God, it's a non-issue now, at least for me.

GERALDINE BINGHAM

We had religious release classes at Hiawatha. Most of my classmates trudged off to Minnehaha Lutheran, while a handful of us went over to the basement of my house across the street, to listen to an elderly lady tell us about the *Catechism*.

A few students stayed in the classrooms, picking no religion to be released to. One former classmate in a different grade school than mine, from a family of committed atheists, said that he "let the teacher do her own thing and wandered out and around the neighborhood during release periods."

Given the differences, though, there still were some traditions that both the Lutheran and Catholic churches throughout south Minneapolis shared. Jell-O, with green grapes and carrot shavings (along with the hot dishes), was served after services at the luncheons and suppers in the basements of all the churches.

14

We went through the railroad overpass and turned west again on East 25th. This was a tough neighborhood then. Less grass, more dirt in front yards. We never got off the streetcar here. Some kid a few rows back shouted out to a girl walking on the sidewalk, "Hubba-hubba-ding-ding, baby you've got…" She turned and gave him the finger. I wasn't sure what it meant, but I didn't think it was nice.

We passed Skol Liquor Store and then angled right onto Minnehaha as it neared the Citizen's Club at Franklin, the sponsor of the summer camp I went to in 1947. My first lake.

I had asked my dad why we had no lake to go to (like Carol Peterson), or a farm (like John Pollard). He said that he did not have a Minnesota background, nor any relatives "up at the lake" or "down on the farm." What was left unsaid was that our family had no extra money to buy or rent a lakeside place. But being a first-time American, he also wanted to see the country.

We started out with short car trips, first Crystal Cave, which had opened in 1942 as a tourist site over in Wisconsin. We graduated to a few overnights on the North Shore. Finally, we scored big with Niagara Falls and California in following years. (On the trip west, in 1951 in the '49 Chevy, my brother and I agreed on a demarcation line that divided up the back seat. Neither was to trespass onto the other's space.)

My one time "up at the lake" at Camp Na-Wau-Kwa (or whatever) was a failure of epic proportions, of which I was not proud. Later, I found out that I was too young (age eight) but had been allowed to go with my nine-year-old brother.

It might have been the first night that I fell out of the top bunk onto the cabin floor. On the second day I was stung by a hornet, which required a trip into the town to see a nice old doctor. By the end of the first week I had been whacked across the nose by a swinging baseball bat (second trip into the town to see the nice old doctor), having sat too close to a kid in the batter's box. (Years later, when my teammates elected me captain of the Roosevelt baseball team, I never let on.) The first day-at-the-beach swim I must not have paid too much attention to the instructions about the "buddy" system and how, at the sound of the lifeguard's whistle, we were to join hands with one's buddy and raise them high. After a short time paddling around I decided to go back to the cabin for a nap. I woke up and went back down to the dock. They were dragging the lake, looking for a boy who had not raised his hand with his buddy when the whistle blew for the "buddy count."

I don't recall writing the mandatory postcard to my mom and dad after the first week. Had one of the counselors been able to do so, it might have been one of those, "Please come and get your kid" messages. In any event, my brother may have sent one that said something like, "Having a good time and they thought Henry drowned," or "…and Henry got into trouble," because I think they drove up for me before the camp ended.

"Na-Wau-Kwa" in Chippewa probably meant something like "Don't ever let that redheaded kid come back onto our sacred grounds."

15

Minnehaha Avenue gave way to Cedar, and the streetcar
came into the Cedar-Riverside neighborhood. We looked out. A
lot of Eastern European immigrants, someone told me. They had
names I couldn't pronounce. We stopped at a light at Riverside.
A car pulled up alongside, windows open. Inside, Patti Page was
singing *Cross over the Bridge*.

The infamous Triangle Bar came up on the right. We began
a slow crawl up the few remaining blocks to Seven Corners.

Bobby jumped from one window to the other, trying to see
if all seven of them — formed by Washington, Cedar, 15th and
2nd — were still there. Streetcars from other south-side lines —
Cedar, Minnehaha, Bloomington — were elbowing their way into
the intersection, even one in from St. Paul.

Courtesy James C. Meyers.

Our car broke free from the pack to turn northwest onto Washington Avenue as it headed downtown.

As we moved through one of the city's more notorious neighborhoods — adult-entertainment — we went by places with "Girls, Girls" and "Follies" on neon signs. Two men were going inside one of them that had an overhead sign: "Nude Dancers." I wondered if they were going to do a lot of French kissing in there. By then I knew that sex was more than just a naked woman; it had a plot. That was the harder part.

A few bums were sleeping against the walls of beat-up old buildings across the street, a huge *Gluek's* billboard hanging crooked off the side of one of them.

> I recall my dad driving us down through the Seven
> Corners area and down Washington Avenue. I peered
> through the car window looking at the drunks lying on
> the sidewalks and the flophouses. It was like another
> universe for me from my provincial Scandinavian family.
>
> PAUL WULKAN

We were at an age when we had yet to make a connection between the stuff those people did inside those places and what Mrs. Bergstrom did back on our block. Bobby's older brother hinted at it once when he said it was all the same thing, but down here on Washington Avenue (where he saw a red light in a window once) it "wasn't very nice" stuff. And usually, when two people "did it," they didn't really love each other, maybe didn't even like each other.

I recall several of us boys browsing through the well-hidden "girlie" magazines at Lockner's Drug store, thinking, "I wonder if I will ever have real sex with a girl before I die?"

PAUL WULKAN

The only naughty stuff for ten- and twelve-year-old eyes up to then were selected pages of the Sears catalog, "Women's Lingerie." Impure thoughts? Other than that we never saw a naked woman standing by a tree as Hopalong Cassidy rode by chasing the bad guys on Saturday morning up at the Falls. But things did get a little sexy, I thought, when we saw Gregory Peck mess around with Jennifer Jones in *Duel in the Sun*. There was no nudity, not even a little bit, in *Vengeance Valley* with Randolph Scott at the Riverview. It would be years before I discovered that if a man was "sleeping" with a woman he was doing something more than sleeping.

The whole sexuality thing was rather pervasive in the lives and minds of all of us. However, it was always over-shadowed with the cloud of guilt. Both we Lutheran and Catholic boys were instilled with the guilt of having such feelings of pleasure and especially acting on it.

PAUL WULKAN

Some others got closer to the stuff than the Sears catalog, closer even than what we read in the last pages of Mickey Spillane's *I, the Jury*.

My friend Connie and I were playing in an empty lot next to a fourplex on the corner and through a basement window saw a naked couple on a couch doing things very foreign to our innocent eyes. Immediately went home and told our parents.

Then the scene was even more "up close and personal" when in sixth grade:

Again, Connie and I were walking to Bancroft, wintertime, when a man approached us on 36th Street. As he walked past us he opened his very long coat and had nothing on. We were a bit traumatized! Went home and told my dad. We got in the car, drove back, and he was still walking, so my dad got a good look at him. He called the police. About a month later Connie and I saw him again at the Dairy Queen across from Bancroft.

JOANNE MAHRE

I remember one time, quite vividly, a man lying on a blanket exposed himself to me and my sister, and us just screaming and running toward the drugstore. (After all, we had to return our bottles.) Luckily for us he didn't chase us. We walked home the long way, through neighborhood blocks, avoiding the lake.

JORUN OLSON

The streetcar kept moving northwest on Washington Street, across from the General Mills facilities and warehouses and the Milwaukee Road and the Soo Line railroad yard, then under the viaduct, up against the passenger terminal on the right. Before we turned at 5th Avenue we saw more sidewalk sleepers, some of them Indians down from the reservations. A few blocks south, we saw the sleek black marble facade of the new *Star and Tribune* building.

We turned back west again and picked up the smell coming from the Old Dutch potato-chip factory opposite the Vendome Hotel and its pool hall. In a few years, I'll get off here, go in and stand by a pool table with a cue stick — lipping a cigarette. We moved on to our stop at 5th and Hennepin, got off and stepped around the cowcatcher to cross over to the corner next to the Loeb Arcade building. We had time, so we ran in and went up the elevator, got off next to the Lakers' offices and looked down over the balcony to the lobby below. It was kind of scary.

Out on the street again we got up to Sixth. Bobby wanted to run across to Shinders' newsstand to look at one of the "girlies" in the back stacks. We didn't have time. Besides, he'd probably run into one of those, "Hey kid! If you peek, you buy" employees. Nor did we have time to go through the pay phones at Dayton's or the Foshay to look for left-behind dimes.

We went up another half block to the "air-cooled" Gopher. Once in the lobby, I saw L.C. Hester off to the side with a few of his friends. (He was in Mr. Wheeler's homeroom at Sanford, same as Cynthia Kersten's.) He didn't seem to recognize me. Just then an usher pointed his flashlight at them, motioning them up to the balcony. He nodded to a man standing next to me, "That's where the colored have to go."

There were no minorities in our neighborhood. However, since my mother worked as a social worker for Hennepin County, she had black friends who came to our home and partook in celebrations like friends do. Our neighbors were doctors. Liberal. They, too, had black friends who visited. Actually, my dad and I marched with Dr. Dahl and his son in a demonstration in Minneapolis once.

SUSAN CODUTI

Portland Avenue at 38th, was just two blocks east of the corner of 4th Avenue and 38th Street. This was a corner of much fascination and a bit of intimidation. This was one of the few black communities in south Minneapolis. Appropriately, Joe's BBQ was on that corner. We did not know anything about redlining in those days, so we only assumed that black folks tethered together in communities as did the Swedes, Norwegians and Germans that we were familiar with. Scandinavians had their ethnic foods, such a lefse and lutefisk, so barbecues made sense in that community.

PAUL WULKAN

No one in our household ever used the "n" word. If referred to at all, they were "colored." But I did have a *Little Black Sambo* book.

JOANNE MAHRE

I didn't know any black kids at all and knew only one Jewish, Italian and Asian kid (and those not close at all).

RONALD PETERSON

The talk at our home was sadly very racist, and I was at Nokomis, a school with no black kids, so I felt very confused on the subject. Race was never discussed in school! When it came to blacks, I said it seemed to me very strange that so many kids and adults used very racist insulting names and jokes when they spoke about them. At that time no real discussions about race in school or church ever took place. My parents did have black friends, but the jokes seemed to be acceptable. But I didn't understand why no one said why this was OK. In my later years I began to see how the subject was addressed, and it seemed to get better. However, so many years of this way of thinking have been passed down in families. Sadly, we have a lot of work to do on this subject.

JUDITH KIBBY

We were pretty much all WASPs with some Catholics thrown in. In high school we had two Hester families who were cousins and black. They were terrific kids. I think a neighbor Donald Erickson (an adopted child) was the only Native American in any of my schools. My high school had one girl whose parents were Chinese. We had no Latinos or Jews that I knew of.

RUTH JOHNSON

Bobby and I went in and saw *King Solomon's Mines*, with Stewart Granger and Deborah Kerr.

After the house lights came back on, I walked back out through the lobby and onto Hennepin. I looked around for Bobby, thought he was behind me. He wasn't.

I blinked in the sunlight and squinted — held it a little longer and then opened my eyes wide. People were walking by with smart phones in clothing styles similar to what I'd seen that morning at the airport, when I arrived for my one-day trip back to my hometown. Okay, I get it. I'm back. I waved down a taxi that took me back to my rental car across from my old house, then drove out to the airport.

Once through TSA security and on the way to my gate, I looked over at a kiosk. An Ethiopian woman was selling framed photos of old Minneapolis scenes. I stared at the one with the streetcar.

The End

Acknowledgments

This book would not have been possible without the honest, candid and humorous anecdotes of twenty-nine former high-school classmates ("storytellers"): Geraldine Bingham, Gloria Blumke (Simmers), James Carlson, Susan Coduti (Morgan), Pat Eide (Ponto), Ronald Eikaas, David Gilman, Paul Gorgos, Charles Gudmunson, Jane Hagen (Hess), John Hrkal, Arloine Hullar (Kallin), Ruth Johnson (Fingerson), Cynthia Kersten (Doran), Judith Kibby (Jennrich), Douglas Larson, Gregory Larson, Joanne Mahre (Haugen), James C. Meyers, Jorun Olson (Robillard), Marlys Olson (Ehrman), Carol Peterson (Repp), Ronald Peterson, Jeanett Pfeifer (Walsh), Judith Slavik (Hrkal), Thomas Stacy, Joseph Steiner, Carol Thorson (Forsberg), and Paul Wulkan. They helped me turn eight "fishing and golfing" memos into the larger story that it is.

In particular, I am grateful to those storytellers who gave of their time and memory to participate in "back seat" interviews on my three return trips to my home town. Joanne Haugen showed me her childhood (Bancroft Elementary School, Powderhorn Park, St. Luke's Lutheran Church, Keller Drug) in June 2016. Over three Minnesota below-zero days later, in December 2016, I discovered the same of Jorun Robillard (Parkway Theater, Wenonah Elementary School, Nokomis Big Beach), Douglas Larson and Thomas "Skip" Stacy (Keewaydin Field, Leola Theater, car-hopping, Dead Man's Cave), and Geraldine Bingham

(St. Helena Catholic Church and School, Little Beach). On my last return trip (April 2017), I heard from Pat Ponto (Longfellow Park, Riverview Theater) and James C. Meyers (Hiawatha Elementary School, streetcars and Minnehaha Park ski jumping).

I wish to give a special thanks to Ms. Ellen Kaufmann (school secretary) and Ms. Lisa Horn (family liaison) of the (now) Hiawatha Community School. They welcomed a small group of us in April 2017 when we arrived unannounced on their doorstep. Ms. Horn spent no less than an hour guiding us through the school, and me through memories of my schoolboy years. The trip down the hallways helped me more accurately describe the same walk that "Bobby" and I take in my story.

My consulting editor, Kathryn Johnson (Kathryn@WriteByYou.com), reviewed several early drafts of the book and provided editorial corrections and invaluable developmental advice as to shape, tone, and content. After her hand, Barbara Scott (Barb@FinalEyes.net) took over my project with enthusiasm and attentiveness, crafting the manuscript into a book.

Sister Mara Faulkner, OSB, professor emerita at the College of St. Benedict *and* a 2010 Minnesota Book Awards finalist *(Going Blind: A Memoir),* was a source of early support and encouragement. She reminded me that "one of the things that memoir lets us do is have a sort of double vision: what we knew/perceived/understood in the past and what we now know that may illuminate the past."

If one wishes to remember their yesterdays with any clarity, visual records of those times assist both the writer and the reader.

I'd like to show my appreciation to Anne Thayer, Eric Mortenson and Fun Fun Cheng, of the Minnesota Historical Society, for their assistance in supplying me with archival photographs. Former classmate Carolann Lavell provided me with valuable photos of the era (as did many of the storytellers), and Greg Brennan Photography improved as best he could many of the sixty-five-plus-year-old scenes (some captured on Kodak Brownies and Hawkeyes).

Finally, a special shout-out to Phillip "Bud" Black (RHS '54), who has been with me on this ride from the beginning, both figuratively and literally. He was an invaluable source of support and anecdotes as an "honorary chauffeur" for me and the storytellers on my return trips. Bud, a storyteller of the highest order, was a "walking encyclopedia" of our south Minneapolis era.

About the Author

After high school, Henry Gallagher left the south Minneapolis neighborhood of his childhood to attend college at St. John's University (Collegeville, Minnesota). He graduated in 1961 with a B.A. in history and that same year received a commission as a second lieutenant in the United States Army. In 1962, he was a part of a large-scale contingent of federal troops sent south to put down a riot spurred by a mob of three thousand whites opposed to the enrollment of the first African-American student, James Meredith, at the University of Mississippi. He was assigned as the officer-in-charge of the security detail for Mr. Meredith, who was facing very real threats to his life. Gallagher's 2012 book, *James Meredith and the Ole Miss Riot: A Soldier's Story,* was a first-person account of that experience.

After his two-year military tour, the transplanted Minnesotan remained "out east" and received a law degree from Georgetown University (Washington, D.C.) in 1971. He retired from a law practice in 2011, and now — with a freckle-free face and a head of hair no longer red — he devotes his time to writing (presently working on a novel set in Vietnam). He lives in Washington, D.C., with his wife, LeChi, a retired law librarian.

Made in the USA
San Bernardino, CA
27 October 2017